EL VALLE DE SILICIO

EL VALLE DE SILICIO

WHY LATIN AMERICA WILL BE THE WORLD'S NEXT TECH BOOM

RISHI KSHATRIYA

NEW DEGREE PRESS

COPYRIGHT © 2018 RISHI KSHATRIYA

All rights reserved.

EL VALLE DE SILICIO

Why Latin America Will be the World's Next Tech Boom

ISBN   *978-1-64137-177-3 Paperback*
         978-1-64137-162-9   Ebook

CONTENTS

INTRODUCTION 7

PART 1

CHAPTER 1. OVERALL REVIEW OF GLOBAL VENTURE CAPITAL 19
CHAPTER 2. ANALYZING THE SUCCESS STORIES 23
CHAPTER 3. THE CONTENDERS FOR THE "NEXT" VC MARKETS 55
CHAPTER 4. WHY LATIN AMERICA 75

PART 2

CHAPTER 5. INSTITUTIONAL NEED 83
CHAPTER 6. DEFENSIBLE INDUSTRIES 111
CHAPTER 7. CULTURAL ALLIANCES 131
CHAPTER 8. CULTURAL SCALABILITY 143
CHAPTER 9. GOVERNMENT SUPPORT 161
CHAPTER 10. INVESTOR SUPPORT 179
CHAPTER 11. ALTERED STRATEGIES 189
CHAPTER 12. RISKS 213

CONCLUSION 231
APPENDIX 237

INTRODUCTION

Before I left China, I was educated that China was the richest, happiest country in the world. So when I arrived in Australia, I thought, "Oh my God, everything is different from what I was told." Since then, I started to think differently.

—JACK MA

* * *

The dotcom crisis rocked the world in 2000.

But there were forty-six million dollars still out there. Forty-six million dollars that were still waiting to be injected into another dotcom—a Latin American dotcom.

After the bubble burst, there was a one-year old company that claimed this capital.

Even after the dotcom crash, even after the world was shocked by the colossal sell-off, the Buenos Aires-based company emerged, slightly wounded but not out. And after the forty-six million, the rest is history.

That company is the e-commerce giant MercadoLibre—the first ever Latin American tech company to be listed on the Nasdaq Stock Market and the region's first ever unicorn.

"In a time when many companies were failing, we realized that there was no more competition, so we had to recognize our mistakes and continue to try new things and experiment ourselves to see what would work; we did not have the capability of hiring outside specialists," says one of the company's early employees now turned venture capitalist.

The scrappiness of the early employees was what got them to where they are today. "One of the main differentiators between MercadoLibre and other companies that went bust was the team," he mentions.

Latin America is a home to founders. It is a home to entrepreneurs.

While many investors were wary and thought about backing out of negotiations after the crash, "they realized the long term value of the company was so great and that the team was, to their surprise, very well capable of running this business, so the term sheet was eventually signed," he recalls. "They knew the future of Latin America was going to be digital."

Just after IPO in August 2007, the global recession hit. But again, the company found a way to emerge. In December of 2007, the first month of the Great Recession, the company's stock soared 82%, and from the span of December 2007 until June 2009, the official lifetime of the recession, the stock returned over 120%.

MercadoLibre has become the poster child of Latin American venture capital.

* * *

Now let's take a look at a typical United States venture capital success story.

In just three years, Groupon went from a startup to accumulating over $1 billion in annual revenue and went public at a $12.7 billion valuation.[1]

Some of the early investors like Accel and New Enterprise Associates clearly saw the future growth potential of this company: disruption.

In today's Silicon Valley ecosystem, the winners in the startup world are the disruptors—the ones that take a traditional industry and completely challenge the norm.

Groupon did just that with corporate promotions. And it became one of the prototypical venture capital success stories of the decade.

* * *

If we look at the current state of global venture capital, the total investment is dominated by the United States, China, and Western Europe—in that order.

---

1 Truong, Alice. "Groupon Is Still the Fastest Company to Reach a Billion-dollar Valuation." Quartz. May 22, 2015. Accessed September 4, 2018. https://qz.com/398090/groupon-still-the-fastest-company-to-reach-a-unicorn-billion-dollar-valuation/.

In 2017 alone, over $76.4 billion in funding was raised in the United States, representing a 10.16% compound annual growth rate over the course of ten years. China raised around $65.5 billion.[2]

Compare such statistics to Latin America, which received $1.1 billion in 2017, more than doubling, however, the $500 million in funding that the region received in 2016.[3]

This growth proves that the Latin American startup culture is growing rapidly but still proves miniscule compared to the United States. However, Latin America is definitely gaining much more recognition than in the past, as total venture capital transactions have increased 46% year over year and aggregate Chinese investments surpassed $1 billion in 2017.[4]

---

2 Yang, Yingzhi. "China's Start-ups Attract Almost Half of World's Venture Capital Investments." South China Morning Post. July 05, 2018. Accessed September 4, 2018. https://www.scmp.com/tech/article/2153798/china-surpasses-north-america-attracting-venture-capital-funding-first-time.

3 Mitchell, Caitlin. "Tech Companies Back New Coalition Created by LAVCA to Support Latin America's Record Breaking Startup Growth." LAVCA | Latin American Private Equity & Venture Capital Association. April 4, 2018. Accessed September 5, 2018. https://lavca.org/press-release/tech-companies-back-new-coalition-created-lavca-support-latin-americas-record-breaking-startup-growth/.

4 Chen, Lulu Yilun. "Chinese Investors Bet on Latin America for Next Tech Gold Rush." Bloomberg.com. March 4, 2018. Accessed September 5, 2018. https://www.bloomberg.com/news/articles/2018-03-04/chinese-startups-export-playbook-to-latin-america-for-new-riches.

Many prominent venture capital firms have started to get their foot in the door in recent years, with big-name investors like Sequoia, Founders Fund, and Accel Partners recently making their first investments in the region.

What these investors are finally seeing is what the initial investors first saw in MercadoLibre in 2000: the digital future of Latin America. The Internet population of Latin America is set to grow from 45% in 2015 to 61% by 2019, surpassing the 400 million mark.[5]

* * *

In these core markets above that have "exploded" over the past two decades, there are four core factors that we observe have led to this "explosion."
- Evolving Industries Driven by Institutional Need
- Cultural Friction
- Institutional Support
- Adaptable Risks that Define How to Navigate the Region's Young Ecosystem

---

5   Gordon, Kyle. "Topic: Internet Usage in Latin America." www.statista.com. 2017. Accessed September 5, 2018. https://www.statista.com/topics/2432/internet-usage-in-latin-america/.

These four components are what I self-proclaim as the "Rishi method" for identifying the prospect of a potential startup boom in an emerging market.

This method can be used as a scoring system, as each component can warrant a maximum of two points with zero meaning no presence of the factor, one meaning some sort of presence, and two meaning the definite presence of the factor. As a result, a region can earn a maximum of eight points through the Rishi method.

Based on my analysis, research, and interviews, I can safely conclude that Latin America is "next."

The stories inside this book involve these institutional industries—from FinTech to agritech to mom-and-pop corner stores.

The cultural friction we will observe involves cross-border corporate and startup partnership and companies scaling all over Latin America and the world.

We will see how governments and venture capitalists alike are transforming the ecosystem day by day and rapidly taking an initiative to scale the region.

Finally, the book will delve into *how* venture capitalists are adapting to the inherent risks of the region and understanding how *not* to invest.

*　*　*

Going back to the earlier story, MercadoLibre clearly provided promise and hope for the rest of Latin America to follow suit some ten to fifteen years ago.

So what happened? Why hasn't Latin America seen the same unprecedented startup growth as Silicon Valley did?

To answer that question, we need to understand how Silicon Valley became the global tech hub.

If you think the United States earns the name "land of opportunity" through its rich past of immigrants searching for a prosperous way of life, then California is that on steroids. Silicon Valley became the startup capital of the world because of its history of "hits-driven" industries.

It all began with the gold rush in the mid-19th century, which brought waves of Americans and foreigners to the West Coast, who all sought riches. Then it was California's oil boom of the early 20th century. Also around this time, Hollywood became the film capital of the world, attracting people and money. In such an environment of "boom or bust" mentality, venture capital was eventually but *accidentally* born.

In 1956, William Shockley recruited a group of scientists to California to create silicon chips, but just a year later, these talented young men left the company and sought to start their own. They became known as the Traitorous Eight. After not being able to find a corporation to hire all of them, they joined forces with Arthur Rock, a banker from New York, who struck a deal with Fairchild Camera to create the startup Fairchild Semiconductor. Eventually, two of the scientists enlisted Rock again to create Intel. In both of these examples, it was the founders that utilized an investor to get their startup off the ground. That's basically how the idea of venture capital began, and it just so happened to start in Northern California.

Venture capital has basically become the modern-day equivalent of the Gold Rush.

Those that "won" the Gold Rush were the ones that found places where others were not mining for gold.

Now, I want to a part of this gold rush. But the issue remains, that in the places where everyone already *is*, I will not win.

I want to pan for gold in Latin America—and win.

* * *

Inside you will hear stories from a Colombian venture capitalist who decided to quit the raising of his next fund to start a B2B lending platform, stories from a cargo delivery founder who bootstrapped his company through Facebook ads, stories from a former executive at Discovery, stories from entrepreneurs and investors in the economically disastrous country of Venezuela, and many more.

Now let me show you why people will soon be rushing for gold in Latin America.

PART 1

CHAPTER 1

OVERALL REVIEW OF GLOBAL VENTURE CAPITAL

―

Before diving into Latin America, we need to first recap the current state of global venture capital.

Investments in startups are thriving—but only in select areas and locations.

In 2015, the United States dominated global venture capital (VC) activity with over $72 billion of invested capital. In second came China at $49 billion, and Europe came third at $14 billion. When we talk about Europe we mainly think of Western Europe, as the United Kingdom, Germany, and

France accounted for over two-thirds of the continent's invested capital.[6]

But if we look at a tech-savvy country like Japan, which ranked seventh in terms of the most capital invested, such a figure only amounted to $800 million.[7] This data points to the fact that the majority of VC activity around the world is concentrated around the top three regions of the United States, China, and Western Europe; the majority of investors have not yet mustered the confidence to look at startups in developing economies.

But does that mean only those regions are capable of creating sustainable startups?

No.

Such statistics only allow us to conclude that those three markets are mature and are either at or past the *disruption* stage of their technologies, which requires the huge sums of money to continue development and secure the "big-boy" exits.

---

6   Pearce, Bryan. *Back to Reality: EY Global Venture Capital Trends 2015*. Ernst & Young. Www.ey.com. 2016. Accessed Summer, 2018. https://www.ey.com/publication/vwluassets/ey-global-venture-capital-trends-2015/$file/ey-global-venture-capital-trends-2015.pdf.
7   Ibid.

To further justify this claim, let's look at the one industry that dominated the receipt of VC dollars for all three of these regions: consumer services—but more specifically, discretionary consumer services. We can more frankly translate this into the "candy" startups and the ones most affected by economic cycles—i.e. the companies engaging in luxury fashion retail, autonomous and shared mobility, etc.

At a macro level, technology is growing and spreading to various corners of the world. However, at a micro level, every region is at a different level of maturity. A classic example is the autonomous vehicle (AV). Companies like Uber, Waymo, Apple, and Tesla have aggressively started testing autonomous vehicles in the U.S. In fact, many articles have touted that the only way Uber can be profitable is by eliminating their business model dependency on drivers. This is only possible if AVs become mainstream. While AVs are relevant in the United States and Europe, many developing markets have not seen the same level of investments in this sector.

The quest now is to find which region not in the top three will be the next one to bring in this influx of capital because once we finally begin to see the "candy" companies dominating the inflow of a region's VC money, then we can deem such a market "mature."

But before this stage, every region once went through an early stage of development in which technology was based around an institutional need and constraints local to that region. And my goal is to find which market is primed for that development phase and in turn ready to eventually evolve into the disruption phase.

To do so, however, we need to delve deeper and understand *how* the current "big three" were able to reach this stage and in turn use such findings to analyze and understand which emerging markets are exhibiting the early signs of such development phase traits.

CHAPTER 2

ANALYZING THE SUCCESS STORIES

In order to properly standardize our analysis of these geographic markets for past, present, and future, we need to establish specific criteria and methods to which we can reference and use to reasonably "score" the regions for identifying a potential startup and tech boom.

As mentioned in the introduction, the criteria that I have identified are based on four core factors that comprise the Rishi method.

Let's recap these components:
- Evolving Industries Driven by Institutional Need
- Cultural Friction

- Institutional Support
- Adaptable Risks that Define How to Navigate the Region's Young Ecosystem

* * *

The first and arguably most important factor for identifying the early stages of a startup boom is if the newly founded companies are being driven by and serving some sort genuine economic need. Before disruption, an economy needs establishment. An easy way to objectively determine this concept is by looking at the industries in which these startups operate—which type of consumer these products and services serve. While the specific data and figures may vary across region and industry, generally, if the total addressable market for the most part defaults to the majority of the general population—rich or poor—, then we can define the given service or good as "institutional." In other words, we must be able to affirmatively answer the question: Does this company improve a bona fide problem that commonly faces the region's citizens?

Once the market for these types of companies is robust and thriving, then a region will enter the disruption phase.

* * *

Cultural friction relates to both the ideas of the ability of the region to strategically partner with foreign investors and companies but also the ability to keep out foreign competitors due to the cultural uniqueness of the market. However, it is imperative that such cultural uniqueness does not prevent the scalability of the local startups. The most obvious way to objectively screen for this component is if in the early stages of the startup phase, the local companies show not only the willingness and ability to join forces with foreign partners but also the mutually positive result of a physical partnership. At the same time, it is important to understand if foreign competitors with similar business models and offerings are able to enter into the market in question, or if the local company is able to successfully restrict entrance due to the targeted nature of its products or services to the specific, local consumers.

* * *

The next factor in the Rishi method is the presence of institutional support. For the most part, these "institutions" comprise of local governments and venture capitalists or general investing groups themselves. In the budding stage of any tech market, startups need outside help to grow, albeit many may say that in the latter stages of development, government is actually the bane of growth. Nevertheless, in the beginning, especially in developing economies, it is crucial that venture capitalists and governments are "founder friendly" and promote growth in the private sector. Such observations can be objectified through the use of government subsidies, tax breaks, and other "pro-small business policies" as well as preferable terms and a more hands-on approach from the investors. In simpler terms, are the outsiders allowing for and promoting the growth of startups?

* * *

The final piece of the puzzle is determining if the inherent "risk" within the region is, for the most part, due to its young tech ecosystem rather than any structural macroeconomic, socioeconomic or political factors. The next step is to analyze the feasibility of adapting to or working around these risks in the short term until the ecosystem matures. We need to understand in what way the region is evolving—are the founders reaping the majority of the gains or are the investors? How is the way we invest different from more established markets like Silicon Valley? Can we understand how *not* to invest? There are a multitude of possible questions to be posed for this final component, which is definitely the most fickle and least objectively determined of the four, but being able to answer and adapt to some of these questions during development will eventually allow for the region to become developed.

* * *

To put the above criteria to the test, let us take a look through the lens of the Rishi method at two of the established markets mentioned in the previous chapter—China and Western Europe—and determine if and how they checked off all four boxes to get to where they are today.

* * *

First, we look at China.

As of May 2018, there were 234 global unicorns, and China has homegrown 120 of them.[8] But what led to such an exponential rise? Let's answer that question by taking a look at the four key factors above.

The transportation industry in China is constantly evolving. A country that was dominated by rail transport with little to no viable personal transportation is now the fastest growing auto market. As the population in China continues to grow and the country continues to spend billions of dollars on

---

8   Nheu, Christopher. "The Secret Behind How Chinese Startups Are Winning – Startup Grind – Medium." Medium. May 01, 2018. Accessed September 5, 2018. https://medium.com/startup-grind/the-secret-behind-how-chinese-startups-are-winning-44876b196626.

infrastructure development, people are realizing the need for personal automobiles but also reliable aftermarket services.

Liheng Li, former senior manager of Alibaba, got into a car accident in 2009. Fortunately, the car was not totaled but still needed some significant repairs. After a thorough online search, he was unable to find a trustworthy mechanic to repair his vehicle. He then turned to friends and family for advice, but again, had no luck. He then personally went door-to-door to repair shops to check out their services, but similar to the previous two methods, could not find any reliable shops.[9]

What Li found was not that all of the repair shops were unreliable but rather that he could not accurately judge the trustworthiness of each shop due to the fact that the personal automobile industry was relatively new in China during this time.

It was at that moment, the light bulb in his head turned on and he obtained the initial idea for Chemayi, which offers car repair services and utilizes a smartphone app platform,

---

9   Schuman, Michael. "Venture Communism: How China Is Building a Start-Up Boom." The New York Times. September 03, 2016. Accessed September 5, 2018. https://www.nytimes.com/2016/09/04/business/international/venture-communism-how-china-is-building-a-start-up-boom.html.

establishing one of China's first customized and trustworthy auto service websites.

In 2013, Li finally put the idea to use when he and three friends set up the company with around $750,000 of their own money. He says, "Henry Ford is gone for so many years, but we are still driving his cars. I felt that I also must pursue a cause that will persist after I'm gone."[10]

Chemayi now operates in most major cities around China, has raised two rounds of funding thus far, and is operating at a strong profit level.

Liheng Li's story is just one example of how China's industries have evolved out of genuine need. Now the auto market is saturated with electric and autonomous vehicles, aiming to disrupt these types of ventures that were set up within the last ten years.

Without companies like Chemayi that inspired China's tech revolution out of a nationwide necessity, the disruptors that make up the majority of those 120 homegrown unicorns would not exist in such prevalence as they do today.

* * *

---

10   Ibid.

Before China, the only real foreign "competitors," in terms of startups, were in the United States, particularly in Silicon Valley.

At the same time, the cultural friction is arguably the most apparent and definite factor of the four in this case. Everyone has seen the Chinese "copycats" of U.S. companies and the hilarious attempts to fool the locals into thinking that some of these companies are authentic, such as Dolce & Banana (my personal favorite), KFG, and Adidos, among many others.

But why have these "copycats" been able to persist?

This may sound bad to outsiders, but in reality, China's lack of protection over intellectual property rights has been a huge contributing factor that has allowed for similar startups to thrive in China. And once they have already established market share, then it is increasingly difficult for foreign companies to gain ground.

Concurrently, the Chinese culture is vastly different from the United States, and to be frank, Chinese citizens prefer Chinese companies. In 2017, 67% of Chinese citizens said they prefer to use more expensive domestic products over imported products[11], and in 2018, over 90% of citizens aged 18 – 29 said they would prefer to use domestic appliance brands over imported brands.[12]

Let us continue with the theme of the auto industry.

Uber vs. Lyft. That is the question in the United States.

But just a few years ago, the question in China was Uber vs. Didi Chuxing. As we can see today, Uber lost this battle and sold its Chinese business to Didi in the middle of 2016. But how did Didi beat Uber, the company that started it all in the ride-sharing industry?

There are two reasons: one is more practical and relates to the fact that Didi won the price cutting war, as Uber was and still is struggling to become profitable domestically, and the other is simply down to the culture.

---

11 Wong, Billy. "China's Middle-Class Consumers: Preferences and Spending Trends." China's Middle-Class Consumers: Preferences and Spending Trends | HKTDC. July 18, 2017. Accessed September 5, 2018. http://economists-pick-research.hktdc.com/business-news/article/Research-Articles/China-s-Middle-Class-Consumers-Preferences-and-Spending-Trends/rp/en/1/1X000000/1X0AAQP5.htm.

12 Li, Jane. "How China's Consumer Patriotism Is Hitting US and International Brands." South China Morning Post. March 22, 2018. Accessed September 5, 2018. https://www.scmp.com/business/china-business/article/2138267/chinas-young-consumers-are-snubbing-foreign-brands-amid.

Cheng Wei, the founder of Didi Chuxing, began his career at Alibaba with an entry-level position. Eventually, he rose through the ranks and reported to an executive named Wang Gang. After being passed up for a promotion, Gang reached out to Wei to brainstorm startup ideas to eventually begin one and leave Alibaba. Ultimately, Wei found inspiration from not only Uber but mainly from Hailo, a UK company that works with the famous London black cabs.[13]

One of the igniting moments for the company came during a snowstorm in Beijing in 2012. As citizens were unable to hail street cabs, they turned to the Didi app to find rides. That was the first time the company surpassed 1,000 orders in a day. Wei mentions, "If it didn't snow that year, maybe Didi wouldn't be here today."[14]

In 2013, Travis Kalanick, then CEO of Uber, and a few other executives toured China to explore the opportunity of expanding Uber into the country. In fact, they visited Didi's offices, which was somewhat of a tense meeting, according to Wei. At one point in the meeting, Wei stood up and confidently drew two lines on a whiteboard—one of which was Uber that started in 2010 and had a steep curve, but the other

---

13   Stone, Brad, and Lulu Yilun Chen. "Uber Slayer: How China's Didi Beat the Ride-Hailing Superpower." Bloomberg.com. October 6, 2016. Accessed September 5, 2018. https://www.bloomberg.com/features/2016-didi-cheng-wei/.

14   Ibid.

was Didi that started a little later and had a steeper curve, which eventually intersected Uber's curve. Wei recalls saying, "Didi would one day overtake Uber, because China's market was so much larger and many of its cities restrict the use and ownership of private cars as a way to manage traffic and pollution." "Travis just smiled," he says.[15]

One of the reasons that Didi won was because of the vast, intimate knowledge of its target market, which at the time was only China. The company had already partnered with Baidu Maps, giving the app immediate geographic data—something Uber needed to organically or strategically fetch on their own.

At the end of the day, Didi just knew its consumers better. The app has a built-in feature that allows passengers to call a driver when drunk and beat Uber to the "pool" option, something so essential in an overcrowded country.

At the same time, like I mentioned, Chinese people like Chinese things more than they like American things; Didi Chuxing is a Chinese name—Uber is not.

As mentioned earlier, eventually Uber gave up and sold their Chinese business to Didi in 2016, but Uber's exit was not so

---

15   Ibid.

abrupt, as the company earlier a strategic alliance with Didi after years of trying to organically grow. Though Didi knew the Chinese market better, Uber's technology was superior, and the strategic alliance allowed Didi to benefit from this, revealing the ability for foreign companies to partner in China—a further incentive for investors and venture capitalists of all kinds.

Even though Didi has begun to expand all over the world, companies like Didi that may be copycats have shown the ability to persist due to the cultural friction that comes with such a unique country like China. And these companies and startups alike have no need to expand outside of the country like Didi because the target market is already so large within the nation of over 1.3 billion people. So the cultural scalability is naturally large.

Examples like Didi show how the cultural friction allowed Chinese startups to attain such accelerated growth in venture capital investment over the recent years.

Now, China has become so advanced that many believe some U.S. firms are starting to become "copycats" of Chinese ideas. A company like LimeBike, a dock-less bike-sharing company based in Silicon Valley, is replicating the very business model of similar companies started in China. Connie Chan, a partner at Andreessen Horowitz, says, "I love this reversal of what

'China copycat' can mean. It no longer just means a Chinese company copying the States, it can mean a U.S. company copying China."[16]

* * *

Perhaps the greatest spur of the Chinese venture capital market has been from the government. "From the central government all the way down to local governments, we have seen a lot of warm support," says Liheng Li.[17]

Li and his team at Chemayi are set up in Hangzhou but more specifically in an area called Dream Town. Subsidized by the government, the businesses in Dream Town enjoy special training benefits, cheap to no rent expenses, cash hand-outs, and many more advantages.

Chemayi pays no rent and utilizes around $450,000 in subsidies for salaries and purchasing equipment for the business.[18]

---

16 Kharpal, Arjun. "Op-Ed: China's Copycat Tech Image Is Fading and That Should Worry US Tech Giants." CNBC. June 13, 2017. Accessed September 5, 2018. https://www.cnbc.com/2017/06/13/china-copycat-tech-image-is-fading-and-that-should-worry-us-giants.html.
17 Schuman, Michael. "Venture Communism: How China Is Building a Start-Up Boom." The New York Times. September 03, 2016. Accessed September 5, 2018. https://www.nytimes.com/2016/09/04/business/international/venture-communism-how-china-is-building-a-start-up-boom.html.
18 Ibid.

At the same time, China's 11th Five-Year Plan, adopted in 2006, arguably led to the "birth" of modern venture capital in China. The plan finally allowed for the development of limited partnerships, which, as we know, are the essential way for venture capitalists and other investors to raise funds and invest in startups. The government's introduction of the LP format was in line with the stated strategy throughout the plan of further developing scientific innovation.

Likewise, since 2008, the government has been injecting capital into startups through "guidance funds," which, according to the National Development and Reform Commission, is defined as "a type of policy fund that is established by the government and managed in market-oriented fashion with the aim to...attract more capital investment in start-ups."[19]

In addition to government promotion and policies, many corporate VC funds from the biggest companies in China like Alibaba, Tencent, Baidu, and Xiaomi, have been active in Chinese startups. Ultimately, these corporate giants do not only help by injecting capital but also by offering their resources for partnership.

---

19   Lu, Ariel, Frank Fu, and Jessie Chen. *China's Venture Capital (VC): Bigger than Silicon Valley's?*INSEAD. Www.insead.edu. April 20, 2018. Accessed September 5, 2018. https://www.insead.edu/sites/default/files/assets/dept/centres/gpei/docs/insead-student-china-venture-capital-apr-2018.pdf.

When Cheng and Didi were first beginning to get off the ground, the company initially received funding from Tencent. Eventually, he realized that the company could utilize Tencent's platform to help increase mobile transactions within the app. Even though Didi was operating at a massive loss, Tencent and other investors were willing to pump money into the company to keep it afloat. In other words, the investors continued to put the startup over quickly returning the fund first.

With both the government and investors on the side of the entrepreneurs, startup founders were allowed to flourish, greatly impacting China's technological rise.

* * *

Speaking of pumping money at negative-profit companies, venture capitalists understood the differences in investing in U.S. and Chinese startups and adapted accordingly.

In such a young ecosystem, obtaining market share was key, especially given that just the domestic market is absolutely massive.

In the United States currently, investors have less of a priority on market share, as they are more responsive to shifts in market factors. For example, in 2015, when the IPO market was at a historic drought—reverting back to near 2012 levels—investors realized that they could not fund further rounds of "price-cutting-for-market-share," so they began to look to altering their portfolio companies' strategy to cutting costs and getting them to cash-flow positive as quickly as possible to be more attractive for M&A exits.

In China, this was not the case. In early 2016, a Singapore-based grocery delivery company called RedMart was operating at a massive loss and was unable to find investors. Nevertheless, the company was acquired by a subsidiary of Alibaba and now enjoys virtually unlimited capital from the e-commerce giant. As a result, the company has been able to cut prices drastically in Southeast Asia and obtain a large chunk of market share.[20]

Investors understood that the ecosystem was very young, but at the same time, with a young ecosystem comes great opportunity for untapped market share. And so, they focused their strategies as such rather than focusing on profit.

Ultimately, investors had to alter their strategies when investing in China, and the example of RedMart is just one of many

---

20 Russell, Jon. "Alibaba's Lazada Confirms Acquisition of Singapore Web Grocery Startup RedMart." TechCrunch. November 01, 2016. Accessed September 5, 2018. https://techcrunch.com/2016/11/01/alibaba-lazada-redmart-confirmed/.

ways venture capital firms have gone about the way they look at Chinese investments. What matters most, however, is that they were able to successfully adapt and that the risks were more of a factor of the country's young ecosystem rather than something more structural about the region.

* * *

Through the analysis above, we can see that the four factors of the Rishi method are able to explain the keys to China's venture capital explosion and how the country was able to emerge as a formidable competitor to the United States in technology today.

* * *

Now, let's put the method to the test again with Western Europe.

One of the biggest, most successful characteristics of European venture capital is the exit market—or at least the drastic uptick in both exit value and total number of exits. In 2012, total exit value amounted to €4.0 billion, but just one year later in 2013, that number shot up to an astounding €14.7

billion! In 2012, the total number of European exits was 362, and in 2017, this figure was 503.[21]

Clearly, something extreme developed in the European tech world. My goal is to look at the foundation that allowed such an explosion to occur.

* * *

The industry that arguably is revolutionizing technology across all geographies, regardless of socioeconomic standing, is FinTech.

From 2012 to 2015, this industry in the United Kingdom was subject to an 83.5% CAGR in terms of total VC investment. Deal value across this period began at €191 million and reached €1.2 billion by 2015.[22]

Founded in 2010, WorldRemit is an international money transfer start-up—known as the WhatsApp of money—and has raised almost $233 million from firms like Accel and

---

21 Hodgson, Leah. "European VC Trends in 8 Charts." PitchBook. July 23, 2018. Accessed September 5, 2018. https://pitchbook.com/news/articles/european-vc-trends-in-8-charts.

22 Sharma, Rahul. *London as a FinTech Hub: What Does the Future Hold?*Deloitte. October 25, 2017. Accessed September 5, 2018. https://events.economia.cz/media/event/17415/files/rahul-sharma_5622d7a.pdf.

Silicon Valley Bank as of August 2018.[23] The company is headquartered in London and was founded by Ismail Ahmed.

After growing up in Somaliland, Ahmed became intrigued by the concept of money transfers after studying economics at the University of London. He recounts, "When I was a school boy, tens of thousands of men crossed the Red Sea to work in the Gulf states [in the oil industry]. It was kind of a gold rush. I became a recipient of remittances from my brother, who was one of the men that went to Saudi Arabia. Then, when I came [to the UK] on a scholarship, I became a sender. So I saw remittances from both sides."[24]

Due to this experience, he understood the business model of the traditional money transfer industry: both the receiver and the sender must go through an agent, which was an added cost in the process. "Often someone who was receiving $100 would travel two or three hours and spend like $15 to get there," he mentions.[25]

---

23 "WorldRemit: Funding Rounds." Crunchbase. Accessed September 5, 2018. https://www.crunchbase.com/organization/worldremit#section-funding-rounds.
24 Featherstone, Emma. "WorldRemit Founder: 'I Lost My Job to Uncover UN Fraud'." The Guardian. January 20, 2017. Accessed September 5, 2018. https://www.theguardian.com/small-business-network/2017/jan/20/worldremit-founder-lost-job-fraud-money-transfers.
25 Ibid.

After finishing his studies, he helped with a United Nations Development Program regarding money transfers. Eventually, he discovered corruption surrounding the remittance program to Somalia and took action by confronting his superior. He recalls, "My boss said if I went and submitted the dossier, I would never be able to work in remittances again, and I took that threat very seriously. I lost my job to uncover the fraud."[26]

It was at this moment that he realized he wanted to start his own mobile money transfer business—one that was not only easy to use but also clean. The application would allow migrant workers to send money to various countries around the world without the need for the middlemen—the agents that physically deal out the money. When he initially created the business plan, he called the application AfricaRemit.[27]

After a four-year battle with the UN regarding the corruption case, he was finally awarded £200,000 in compensation for how he had been treated throughout the deal and later used this money to launch the business. "I received the letter from the UN ethics committee mid-December, and a few days later, I incorporated the company," he says.[28]

---

26 Ibid.
27 Ibid.
28 Ibid.

Ahmed delves further into the institutional nature of the application: "The unbanked people have for the first time access to a digital store where they can put their money rather than having to put it under the mattress. The innovation that's happening in emerging economies is driving the switch to digital. Increasing numbers of people have obtained low end smartphones, sub $50."[29]

Even more important is that the application targets migrants, who tend to frequently send sums of money back home. London and the United Kingdom make so much sense for an application like this because of the concentrated amount of immigrants from a diverse set of geographies that frequently come and settle down in search of better opportunities.

This phenomenon of sending money home is by no means new but was typically dominated by cash payments, increasing the risk of the money not even reaching the home country as well as money laundering and other illegal activity. The switch to mobile money creates a paper trail and is a more secure way to confidently send money back home.

---

29 Williams-Grut, Oscar. "Here's Why WorldRemit Is worth £320 Million - It's Building the WhatsApp of Money." Business Insider. June 15, 2015. Accessed September 5, 2018. https://www.businessinsider.com/worldremit-founder-ismail-ahmed-mobile-wallets-moneyconf-500-million-valuation-2015-6.

Now, Ahmed eyes further global expansion and incorporation, as the company operates in over 130 countries as of 2017.[30]

Companies like WorldRemit emerged in the earlier part of the 2010s, which led to the massive exit expansion that began in 2013. Through stories like Ahmed's, these FinTech companies have been started out of genuine need of the citizens, which has led to the initial boom and is now leading into the disruptors we see across industries in Western Europe.

* * *

One of the main benefits of investing in the United Kingdom from foreign venture capitalists' point of view is that everything is already in English. Likewise, the United Kingdom has typically been known as a bridge for international expansion to both Europe and around the world. In this regard, it does seem easier for foreign companies to strategically partner and expand within Europe, but at the same time, Europe is generally a hodgepodge of various cultures and languages with relatively small domestic markets, which are factors that could stymie massive scale and growth opportunities.

---

30 Featherstone, Emma. "WorldRemit Founder: 'I Lost My Job to Uncover UN Fraud'." The Guardian. January 20, 2017. Accessed September 5, 2018. https://www.theguardian.com/small-business-network/2017/jan/20/worldremit-founder-lost-job-fraud-money-transfers.

It is definitely quite easy to surpass any major cultural barriers in the United Kingdom due to the language, but such a situation may not be as simple in other European countries.

At the same time, organizations like the Startup Europe Partnership (SEP) have helped create solutions to promote a more integrated technological environment for companies across the continent.

One example of this manifestation is through Berlin-based Uberall. Founded in 2012, the company brings together local businesses and customers by ensuring companies are found across directories, applications, GPS devices and maps with consistent profiles. In essence, not only is Uberall working with SEP to become further integrated across Europe but it is also operating around a business model that connects consumers and businesses from different countries around the continent.

Co-founder Sebastiaan Roebroek mentions, "Like everyone else, I always enjoyed finding new places – whether in my adopted home of Berlin, or somewhere new entirely – and I knew the problem of finding great places to eat or drink, or to find businesses I needed, given that sites and magazines always seemed to recommend the same handful to go to. While these cafes or bars were fun to visit, I always felt that there was a better model out there for consumers, and a better way to get people to go to businesses with real local expertise and presence."[31]

After realizing this problem, he and his colleague David Federhen set out to create a solution. The company eventually grew to over 100 employees with Fortune 500 clients such as The Marriott Hotel Group and Vodafone. The company soon opened another location in San Francisco. The company also partnered with Yelp in 2017 to expand coverage and quality in the United States.[32]

Uberall has shown not only the ability to partner but also the cultural scalability of European startups. However, the fact that an organization like SEP exists and was needed by Uberall reveals to us the inherent difficulty of trying to create a naturally pan-European company from the onset.

The cultural friction is definitely enough within each individual country to keep out foreign competitors, but at the same time, the target markets are not big enough to both create substantial exits and in turn attract big-name foreign investors; due to the small individual populations of each country, it is increasingly difficult to expand outside the home country.

---

31 Roebroek, Sebastiaan. "Growth Story: How German Startup Uberall Became the Go-to Solution for Location Listings." The Next Web. July 05, 2017. Accessed September 5, 2018. https://thenextweb.com/insider/2017/07/05/uberall-growth/.

32 Ibid.

Programs like the Startup Europe Partnership have helped create this cross-European integration, but the reason why Europe experienced a tech boom was not necessarily due to the fact that the startups were able to culturally scale but rather due to the general idea that Europe was already a more developed economy on other fronts outside of technology—infrastructure, politics, disposable income, etc.

* * *

While the institutional support, especially in terms of government support, may be a little more variable from country to country due to the fact that each government has separate policies for its respective countries, the governments of Western Europe have been collectively promoting startup development for years.

The first country to really experience this government support was the United Kingdom, as the government enacted entrepreneur-friendly Startup Visas, tax breaks for angel investments, and Entrepreneurs' Relief, which lets startup employees only pay 10% capital gains tax on qualifying assets.[33]

---

33 Butcher, Mike. "London's Tech Boom Is More Than Just Hype, The Hard Numbers Say So." TechCrunch. September 20, 2014. Accessed September 5, 2018. https://techcrunch.com/2014/09/20/londons-tech-boom-is-more-than-just-hype-the-hard-numbers-say-so/.

In Germany, the government began to take a more active role in the startup community in 2012 through the establishment of the European Angels Fund, which matches a certain percentage of angel investments. The fund works through a grant called INVEST, which provides angels with a grant of 20% of the investment amount in startups, allowing the startups to scale quicker and larger.[34]

France has begun to enact similar government policies recently, but the country made strides in prior years through the notion of investor support.

Partech Ventures, headquartered in San Francisco but with an office and significant presence in France, opened a co-working space in Paris called Partech Shaker for its portfolio companies. One of the main reasons why the venture capital firm saw this space as a beneficial investment was the proximity to Fortune 500 companies in the city of Paris. "For big businesses it's not just about buying companies, it's also about access to the best brains," argues Romain Lavault, a general partner at Partech Ventures.[35] Not only does the

---

34 Bathke, Benjamin. "Insights into Germany's Startup Scene | DW | 18.10.2017." DW.COM. October 18, 2017. Accessed October 13, 2018. https://www.dw.com/en/insights-into-germanys-startup-scene-entrepreneurship-funding-venture-capital-investing-expansion/a-40993536.

35 Ranger, Steve. "Startup Republic: How France Reinvented Itself for the 21st Century by Wooing Entrepreneurs to Paris." TechRepublic. Accessed September 5, 2018. https://www.techrepublic.

space allow for an easier path to exit through acquisition due to the potential for facilitated dialogue, but it also exists so that the Fortune 500 companies have access to the talented entrepreneurs of these startups as well. Romain elaborates, "In my time, most of my class would go to work in banking or consulting and that's it. Now if you are a top student of the class, you want to be an entrepreneur, you want to create your own job, and so that had become a problem for corporates—they can't recruit anymore. That's also why we see these corporates getting closer and closer to startups, because they realize this is the only way to acquire talent."[36]

In the earlier part of the decade, the governments and investors of Western Europe started to promote startups and create favorable policies around developing the technological future of these nations, attracting more and more innovative startups and in turn venture capital firms to the region.

* * *

One large risk in the European ecosystem during the early stages of its technological inception was simply a lack of talent in comparison with its counterparts in the United States and China, despite the status of Western Europe's economies

---

com/article/startup-republic-how-france-reinvented-itself-for-the-21st-century-by-wooing-entrepreneurs-to-paris/.

36 Ibid.

as "developed." When the technological boom did not occur in the early 2000s like in the United States, many credited such a situation to a lack of employee talent. "Europe is on the cusp of greatness, but risks coming short of building companies the size of Amazon, Facebook, and Google if it cannot compete for the talent it needs," says Neil Rimer, founding partner of Index Ventures.[37]

European governments have been lax on the specifics regarding startup operations, such as factors like employee ownership. Research has shown that on average, U.S. employees now own twice as much of their respective startups than their counterparts in Europe. However, the team at Index Ventures has begun to create a handbook for policymakers and entrepreneurs that would outline the best way to go about leveling the playing field in Europe. "Access to talent is the single most important ingredient for creating transformative tech companies, which is why we are calling on European governments to help level the playing field for our ambitious entrepreneurs by creating the right conditions to support and incentivise employee ownership. Attracting the best talent is the biggest focus for all entrepreneurs and should be the singular focus of all governments who seek to support

---

37 Nair, Praseeda. "Are European Tech Start-ups Being Held Back by Lower 'reward for Risk'?" Growth Business. November 30, 2017. Accessed September 5, 2018. https://www.growthbusiness.co.uk/european-tech-start-ups-lower-reward-for-risk-2553041/.

innovation, entrepreneurialism and job growth," says Martin Mignot, a partner at Index.[38]

The main point to note is that the lack of laws surrounding employee ownership and stock option rights is due to the fact that the local governments had not dealt with such policies before—the ecosystem was young. In order to combat such a predicament, Index launched a program called OptionPlan, which allows entrepreneurs to design their own stock option plans for their companies.

Employee ownership is a very underrated concept when it comes to a successful startup. If someone were to sit in on a term sheet discussion with a venture capital firm and a founder, they would almost always witness a question regarding the increasing of or the willingness to increase the employee stock option pool.

But why? Because increasing the option pool attracts talented employees to the startup by letting them know that they would be valued and essential members of the team.

Firms like Index have been able to alter their strategies by allowing portfolio companies to construct their own option

---

38 Ibid.

pools rather than dealing with the various individual governments of each European country.

On the other hand, arguably the biggest risk when navigating Europe is the decentralization of both startups and governments and figuring out how to navigate each country to successfully scale and reach a considerable exit.

In the United States, beginning a company automatically gives the founder access to an English-speaking market of over 327 million people.[39] In contrast, starting a company in France gives access to a population of just 65 million people.[40]

I would love to say that this is an adaptable risk defined by a young ecosystem, but frankly, it is not and will never truly be "adaptable." The general idea of the EU and its integration certainly helps but the cultures and languages will always be vastly different. So for that reason, I cannot say that the Rishi method helps explain this fourth factor completely, but maybe that is why Western Europe is still a distant third place from the United States and China.

---

39 "U.S. Population (LIVE)." U.S. Population (2018) - Worldometers. Accessed October 13, 2018. http://www.worldometers.info/world-population/us-population/.

40 "France Population 2018." France Population 2018 (Demographics, Maps, Graphs). Accessed October 13, 2018. http://worldpopulationreview.com/countries/france-population/.

To a certain extent, the method does shed some light regarding risks, such as with the option pool and Index's solution to this problem, but overall, the variation of cultures will always persist.

* * *

Looking back at our two "case studies," we can see that for the most part, the Rishi method does explain how these two regions were able to create a foundation that led to the tech boom defined by the total venture capital investment numbers highlighted in the previous chapter.

I believe it is fair to score these regions according to the method and determine how well the regions fit the criteria. As mentioned in the introduction, each geographical region can obtain a maximum of two points per component, with eight points being the maximum.

For China, I would assign a perfect eight. The country checked off all the boxes completely, which is why they have almost caught up to and soon will catch up to the United States in terms of total capital invested.

For Western Europe, I would assign a score of six out of eight. The region definitely hits the mark on the evolving industries driven by institutional need and the institutional support fronts but comes short on the cultural friction and adaptable risks due to a young ecosystem factors. To a certain extent, for the latter two factors, the region does meet part of the criteria but the great variation between each country is what holds back one of the two points for each.

* * *

The Rishi method is not one hundred percent perfect but is nevertheless a good proxy for initially determining the workings of a budding tech boom for any young tech ecosystem.

With that said, enough of what has happened—let's dive into the regions that could be next.

CHAPTER 3

THE CONTENDERS FOR THE "NEXT" VC MARKETS

After looking at China and Western Europe's success through the lens of the Rishi method, we now understand the details of the four criteria and can analyze current emerging markets as such.

By the title of this book, it is pretty easy to figure out that I believe Latin America will be the "next" big venture capital market, but it is only fair to first take a look at the other main challengers and score them accordingly.

The top three opponents of Latin America that experts generally regard as possible candidates for the world's next tech boom are Sub-Saharan Africa, the Middle East, and Southeast Asia.

**

Sub-Saharan Africa consists of relatively large geography—it basically encompasses every African country save the whole top row (Western Sahara, Morocco, Algeria, Tunisia, Libya, and Egypt).

Similar to the Western Europe story, the region is definitely experiencing a FinTech revolution, which on the surface level, seems to check off the evolving industries criteria.

M-Pesa is arguably the most well known FinTech startup that many African citizens use and was launched by Safaricom, a Kenyan mobile operator backed by Vodafone.

The mobile payments company was launched in 2007 and currently has over 30 million users in 10 countries. The company processed over 6 billion transactions in 2016 alone![41]

---

41 Monks, Kieron. "M-Pesa: Kenya's Mobile Success Story Turns 10." CNN. February 24, 2017. Accessed September 6, 2018. https://www.cnn.com/2017/02/21/africa/mpesa-10th-anniversary/index.html.

Clearly, the application, which is used by citizens in countries like Kenya, Ghana, and Mozambique, has created a formula for success in an area with an incredibly large market (over 1.2 billion people!).[42]

In 2002, British engineers and organizations in the United Kingdom documented that many citizens from Ghana, Botswana, and Uganda, had been using credit for "pay-as-you-go" mobile phones, as a proxy for money transfer.[43] Thus, they determined that there was clearly a need for a more efficient money transfer system.

M-Pesa's success is a testament to the industries in Africa that clearly have an institutional need for the continent's traditional industries. The only caveat is that the research behind the company was developed and discovered by engineers in the United Kingdom.

Similar to this situation, Cobby Amoah stood up on stage at the Dallas Entrepreneur Center pitching his company Obaa

---

42 Knowles, Daniel. *The 1.2 Billion Opportunity*. The Economist. The Economist. April 16, 2016. Accessed September 6, 2018. http://www.economist.com/sites/default/files/20160416_africa.pdf.

43 McKemey, Kevin, Nigel Scott, David Souter, Thomas Afullo, Richard Kibombo, and O. Sakyi-Dawson. *Innovative Demand Models for Telecommunications Services*. Department for International Development. September 2003. Accessed September 6, 2018. https://assets.publishing.service.gov.uk/media/57a08d10e5274a27b20015e3/2936_R8069_FinalReport.pdf.

to a panel of judges to win a grant to further develop the company. The Ghana native's company is focused on providing an easier, more sophisticated messaging system for healthcare professionals in his home country.

As he stood on stage telling his story of growing up in the sub-Saharan African country, he recalled his realization of how dire the need was for quality healthcare in his home country and his mission to come to the Massachusetts Institute of Technology to create the future of his nation.

He cited the lack of resources in Ghana as the reason that he needed to come to the United States to develop the platform and then eventually return to scale the company further.

M-Pesa was founded in 2007, and Obaa was founded in 2015, but what matters and what has not changed is the idea of the founders and developers still needing resources from outside the continent to create innovative companies.

Some could say that outsourcing the resources and development could be an adaptable risk, but not all investors and founders can sustainably do so; at some point, to maintain economic efficiency, more development needs to occur domestically.

While the culture is very unique and can keep out foreign competitors, the region still has yet to show an ability to partner, mainly through the fact that investors and foreign companies have not shown substantial willingness to enter the region compared to other places around the world.

At the same time, the government, while still improving, has not yet allowed the private sector to autonomously "build" enough to generate innovation.

There are institutional industries primed to evolve, but the region is still inhibited by a lack of resources, which is why we cannot say that the region will be "next." Eventually, I believe all regions of the world will experience some sort of major tech boom, but sub-Saharan Africa will not be the one to make the headlines next. The ecosystem is still too young.

Out of eight points, sub-Saharan Africa receives four.

* * *

The Middle East is the region we will look at next.

Middle East Venture Partners (MEVP), a venture capital firm headquartered in Dubai, is the largest firm by fund size in the

Middle East.⁴⁴ CEO Walid Hanna has definitely witnessed the development of the Middle East's venture capital market over the years but still believes that the region has years to go before people can truly say that the Middle East has caught up to more technologically advanced regions.

Hanna founded MEVP in 2010, and his first fund size was $10 million.⁴⁵ Yes, in an era where Sequoia raised a $1 billion fund at the end of 2009⁴⁶, the first ever fund closed in the MENA region was just $10 million.

In September of 2017, the firm raised $250 million for its third fund, demonstrating not only the rapid success over seven years but also the potential of the MENA region in the years to come. Hanna mentions, "We were really one of the first ones in this VC space. The number, the quantity and the quality of start-ups that we used to see at that time was small, and also very poor in quality. Seven years later, at the

---

44 Debusmann, Bernd, Jr. "Middle East Venture Partners: Investing in the Future of Tech." ArabianBusiness.com. January 16, 2018. Accessed September 7, 2018. https://www.arabianbusiness.com/startup/387400-middle-east-venture-partners-investing-in-the-future-of-tech.
45 Ibid.
46 Bowman, Matt. "Sequoia Raising $1 Billion Umbrella Fund." VatorNews. December 22, 2009. Accessed October 13, 2018. http://vator.tv/news/2009-12-22-sequoia-raising-1-billion-umbrella-fund.

end of 2017, the numbers are completely different, and the quality is also much higher."[47]

The company's first and most successful exit was a company called Shahiya, an Arabic food-focused social website. The company grew to the largest of its kind in the region and was acquired by Japan-based Cookpad in 2014 for $13.5 million. This represented a 6x cash-on-cash multiple on MEVP's original investment just two years prior.[48]

"The interesting part is that Cookpad were on a consolidation spree on a global level, so they acquired the Spanish equivalent, the Indonesian equivalent and the Arabic-language equivalent. By building a MENA market leader in any vertical, you will be acquired. That's exactly our investment philosophy. In whatever vertical we look at within the tech sector, we want to build the number one company," affirms Hanna.[49]

Some of the other "number ones" that Hanna lists are Altibbi, an Arabic WebMD copycat, Lamsa, a website for children's

---

47 Debusmann, Bernd, Jr. "Middle East Venture Partners: Investing in the Future of Tech." ArabianBusiness.com. January 16, 2018. Accessed September 7, 2018. https://www.arabianbusiness.com/startup/387400-middle-east-venture-partners-investing-in-the-future-of-tech.
48 Ibid.
49 Ibid.

entertainment, and Anghami, an online marketplace for consumers to interact with music labels and artists.

What is interesting is if we analyze these industries in MEVP's portfolio. For the most part, these companies are not necessarily institutional—they are disruptive in nature. The issue is that these industry leaders, especially in countries where industries are dominated by state-owned companies, obtain that status and then stay as the only major players in the industry. In other words, there is not a lot of opportunity for multiple companies in the same industry to generate similar returns to the "number ones."

One of the most successful exits in the region came in March of 2017 when Souq, an online retail e-commerce website, was acquired by Amazon for $580 million.[50]

In the Middle East at this point in time, only the "number ones" had the potential of getting acquired because the ecosystem, for the most part, had never had a history of innovation across industries until the beginning of the 2010s.

---

50 Russell, Jon. "Amazon Completes Its Acquisition of Middle Eastern E-commerce Firm Souq." TechCrunch. July 03, 2017. Accessed October 13, 2018. https://techcrunch.com/2017/07/03/amazon-souq-com-completed/.

Just by looking at the acquisitions, the region's main exits have come through foreign companies acquiring their Arabic copycat version, which is a testament to the positive cultural friction aspect of the region but also a factor of concern for the innovation coming from deep-rooted, institutional industries.

Speaking of exits, acquisition is basically the only feasible path, according to Souhail Khoury of Berytech in Lebanon. He elaborates, "Exits have not been very common; the absence of structures that allow IPOs and the relatively short period since the boom of VC funding are the major bottlenecks. Most investors in the MENA are anticipating a horizon of 8-9 years from investment to exit while the Lebanese Central Bank Circular 331 gives funds a 7-year investment mandate. The long exit cycles has been a huge deterrent for wealthy individuals, family offices and other investors looking for more liquid investments."[51]

While the artificial intelligence strategies the United Arab Emirates has enacted to innovate various sectors across the country seem promising, the fact that the government has not yet caught up to improving structures for venture

---

51 Khoury, Souhail. "VC Capital in MENA and Lebanon : Learnings from the Middle East Investment Summit." Medium. May 17, 2018. Accessed September 7, 2018. https://medium.com/@souhailk/vc-capital-in-mena-and-lebanon-learnings-from-the-middle-east-investment-summit-55221c216e31.

capitalists is a great deterrent for investors. I am certain that such measures will improve in the future, but right now, the policies are not as robust as those of other emerging markets and as the markets in the couple of years leading up to the booms of China and Western Europe.

Hanna lists that one of the main shortcomings of the region is the lack of R&D centers in comparison to the United States. He explains, "It's about quantity, quality, and time. If we had research and R&D centers within universities, we would gain in all these areas. The best entrepreneurs we invest in today are an average of 38 years-old. In the US, it's much younger than that. Why? It's because they [the entrepreneurs in the US] have R&D centers, grants and funding. They're part of larger accelerators like Techstars and Y Combinator that we don't really have."[52]

"We're lagging behind by many years... The number of computer engineers and computer science graduates out of the UAE and Saudi Arabia is negligible. You find much more in countries like Egypt and the Levant. In the GCC [Gulf Cooperation Council], it's definitely not good on that side.

---

52 Debusmann, Bernd, Jr. "Middle East Venture Partners: Investing in the Future of Tech." ArabianBusiness.com. January 16, 2018. Accessed September 7, 2018. https://www.arabianbusiness.com/startup/387400-middle-east-venture-partners-investing-in-the-future-of-tech.

What usually happens is that we import those brains," Hanna mentions.[53]

The lack of homegrown R&D and the need to externally develop or import resources is similar to Africa's predicament, but is definitely an adaptable risk. Unfortunately, such a risk cannot be adapted in a quick enough time span to catch up to other emerging markets like that of Latin America.

For the Middle East, the Rishi method delivers the region a score of three out of eight.

* * *

Now, we jump to what is probably Latin America's greatest competitor—Southeast Asia (not including China). Think of Singapore, Indonesia, Vietnam, Thailand, Malaysia, the Philippines, etc.

In 2017, the region managed to attract $7.86 billion from investors.[54] This was a considerably greater amount than the $1 billion Latin America pulled in, and on the surface, implies that Southeast Asia is going to beat Latin America.

---

53 Ibid.
54 Balea, Judith. "Southeast Asia Sees Record Startup Funding in 2017." Tech in Asia - Connecting Asia's Startup Ecosystem. January 25, 2018. Accessed September 7, 2018. https://www.techinasia.com/southeast-asia-sees-record-startup-funding-2017.

This statistic gives all the proof we need to show that Southeast Asia is booming, as it is highly regarded by many experts as the "next" big venture capital market. So with that in mind, there are many positives—the governments are all very pro-business and the risks are certainly adaptable—but I will not focus on the "positives."

The hard and actually interesting part is proving why these experts are wrong. So let's see why.

Until 2007, the golden child of Southeast Asia's startup ecosystem was a Singaporean company called Creative Labs. The company was founded in 1981 and became incredibly successful for manufacturing MP3 players before the iPod. Eventually, the product went out of fashion and the company was delisted from the NASDAQ in 2007.[55]

Until the middle of the 2000s, Southeast Asia's startup environment was defined by hardware, particularly semiconductors. Eventually, the region made a favorable and much needed shift to software.

---

55   Zhu, Juliet. "How to Hunt Unicorns in Southeast Asia: Explains a Venture Capitalist – KrASIA." Kr-Asia. June 20, 2018. Accessed September 8, 2018. https://kr-asia.com/how-to-hunt-unicorns-in-southeast-asia-explains-a-venture-capitalist/.

Juliet Zhu of Fosun RZ Capital recalls that startup investment began to pick up around 2011: "As the tourism industry flourished, the local investment circle was joined by what was then called 'tourist angels,' who flew to Bali for vacation several times a month and, as a sideline activity, made investments and attended board meetings during their stay."[56]

* * *

From basically the onset, Southeast Asia's technology and startups became defined by the disruptor-type companies we see today—e-commerce and games.

Rocket Internet, launched first in Europe, began to launch e-commerce clones around the world and eventually created Lazada in Singapore in 2012. To a certain extent, the service was popular, and the company maintained a high gross merchandise volume (GMV), which is an indicator of total sales dollar value for merchandise sold over a certain time frame. However, there came a point where ad spend grew higher than GMV.[57] In other words, Lazada was focused on market share and obtaining growth rather than profitability. Eventually, Alibaba bought the company in order to inject capital to maintain this strategy.

---

56 Ibid.
57 Ibid.

Since these types of businesses were not as robustly developed due to the young market, the users tried to find loopholes.

For example, Zhu recounts a comical instance where users of Foodpanda, a food delivery platform, could make money themselves: "By selling pancakes to themselves on the food delivery platform Foodpanda, people could earn money from both the coupons offered to users and the subsidies granted to merchants. After burning $300 million, Foodpanda's Southeast Asia business split into several divisions, which were then sold at low prices."[58]

Games startups are also very popular in the region, as Garena, a game title distributor, IPO'ed in October of 2017 and has been very successful.

I do believe that these types of companies will persist and, to an extent, remain very successful in the region, but because the region basically emerged with these technologies from inception, they will basically be the only types of companies that will generate the big bucks.

The reason why users were able to find loopholes in the technology of the online platforms was because companies tried to adopt the disruptor business model before the region's

---

58   Ibid.

staple industries began to become defined by technology. The citizens had not yet become accustomed to technology consuming their everyday lives. Now that the region has become defined by the disruptor phase in only certain segments, investors will shy away from deploying capital into the staple industries because those will not generate as high of a potential exit as the few disruptors out there.

The reason why these staple industries are so important is that the unique industries to each region are what are going to eventually drive the scale and value-add of a region to the rest of the world; these institutional industries are what will differentiate and give a competitive advantage to the region as opposed to other countries.

When a region immediately starts to begin the foundation of its technological ecosystem on established disruptors (aka copycats—just in a different language), the founders and investors must rely on the cultural friction to keep out competitors and hope that the region's scale is large enough to sustain a sizable exit or sustained financial profile.

When a company is a copycat, there is nowhere else to really go outside the region because, clearly, the company being copied has already established itself elsewhere.

By this logic, investors are hoping that the cultural friction and sizable target market of Southeast Asia will create strong returns, but the cultural friction may not be as strong as people think.

There is, however, a shining light in Southeast Asia: FinTech is incredibly popular in the region, which we have seen is a major plus for any emerging market that incorporates this specific industry into the lives of its citizens.

Like Silicon Valley's pivot from hardware to software, it is not impossible for a region to expand and redefine its technological ecosystem, but such an about-face takes time. In this regard, Southeast Asia will have success and eventually have its natural, local industries become defined by technology and create sustainable growth for the region—it just may not be as soon as people think.

* * *

In 2017, 71% of all venture funding in Southeast Asia was in Singapore, 22% in Indonesia, 3% in Malaysia, and 2% in Thailand.[59]

---

59   Balea, Judith. "Southeast Asia Sees Record Startup Funding in 2017." Tech in Asia - Connecting Asia's Startup Ecosystem. January 25, 2018. Accessed September 7, 2018. https://www.techinasia.com/southeast-asia-sees-record-startup-funding-2017.

Most of the funding is concentrated in Singapore because not only is the country the "tech hub" of Southeast Asia, but it also is the most "Western," or applicable to other developed parts of the world. Perhaps that is how Singapore became the region's tech hub.

The issue is that the region is very culturally divided, similar to Europe. Zhu elaborates, "The market there may seem large, but the region is in fact divided into independent communities with different religions, customs and laws. This has become a major obstacle keeping businesses from expanding across the region. The fact that spending power varies from country to country and even from city to city means that companies must constantly redefine their target markets, familiarise themselves with the local business environment and competitive landscape, and adjust their customer acquisition methods and management models."[60]

Zhu recalls her time working with a popular luxury resale platform in Singapore that actually gave up on the rest of Southeast Asia and eventually targeted Hong Kong and Taiwan for its expansion. The company initially tried utilizing similar advertising slogans across the countries but found

---

60 Zhu, Juliet. "How to Hunt Unicorns in Southeast Asia: Explains a Venture Capitalist – KrASIA." Kr-Asia. June 20, 2018. Accessed September 8, 2018. https://kr-asia.com/how-to-hunt-unicorns-in-southeast-asia-explains-a-venture-capitalist/.

that while one slogan was received relatively normally in Thailand, it was actually considered blasphemous in Indonesia. On the operations side, programmers and employees interpreted the word "deadline" differently, and salespeople had to attract customers in each country in completely different ways.[61]

While many of these tribulations can be solved by more extensive market research, such a task is just more time and money spent away from actually trying to scale the operations of the business. What matters is that in Southeast Asia, startups must approach each market differently, creating another hassle for the entrepreneurs and the venture capitalists. An adaptable risk here would be to simply enlist local companies to partner, which is certainly viable, but again, this is just more valuable money and market share given up.

The region is much more culturally fractious than one can tell from first glance.

If the region is defined by copycats, and the copycats cannot regionally scale, then the geographic market cannot grow—at least not as rapidly as others.

---

61   Ibid.

As of October 2018, Singapore's population is 6 million, Indonesia is at 267 million, Malaysia is at 32 million, and Thailand is around 69 million.[62]

Countries like Indonesia and Thailand certainly have large enough populations to remain sustainable target markets individually, so I am by no means saying that the large investments of recent years in Southeast Asia is a bubble.

The issue is that the region will have a tough time growing rapidly enough to break the true "boom" threshold before other regions do.

Southeast Asia, I believe, is certainly primed for technological success, but it will not be "next."

Latin America's ecosystem is currently checking off all of the four boxes and will eventually surpass the investment in Southeast Asia in a few years' time.

Southeast Asia receives a five out of eight.

---

62 "South-Eastern Asia Population (LIVE)." Population of South-Eastern Asia (2018) - Worldometers. October 14, 2018. Accessed October 14, 2018. http://www.worldometers.info/world-population/south-eastern-asia-population/.

CHAPTER 4

WHY LATIN AMERICA

Now that we have looked at Latin America's competitors, let's take a look at the Latin America region and preview the remaining part of this book.

Latin America truly does check off all the boxes.

First and foremost, the region has the institutional industries that not only are driving the world's general tech boom in FinTech but also has the differentiated sectors such as agri-tech, mining, and other niche areas.

FinTech is currently the heart of Latin America's initial tech revolution, as a company called Nubank is one of the crown jewels of Latin America's FinTech revolution.

As we have seen with Western Europe, FinTech is a staple industry that can greatly spark an overall tech boom because it allows those who have previously not had access to technology the power to utilize applications for their personal finances. FinTech allows the denizens of the region to begin to use technology for everyday applications.

At the same time, there are plenty of other differentiated and scalable industries in Latin America like agritech and "mining-tech" that have begun to attract investors and revolutionize the traditional carriers of Latin American economies.

Latin America also is known for "impact investments," meaning an investment defined by some sort of social mission. On the surface, this seems a bit wishy-washy and does not seem like anything that could actually help start a tech boom, but again, there are genuine needs behind such investments. I actually believe that these impact investments are to an extent less risky than traditional investments for reasons I will delve into in the next section of the book.

* * *

Of course, another one of Latin America's crown jewels is MercadoLibre, the Amazon of the region, but these types of disruptors actually have the benefit of true cultural friction to keep out companies like Amazon, unlike in Southeast Asia.

At the same time, the region has shown a willingness to partner from the corporate all the way down to the startup level, providing foreign investors with an incentive to inject capital in years down the line; from a foreigner's point of view, doing business in Latin America is not as difficult as it may seem.

In the next few chapters, we will delve into examples and stories of companies that have been able to achieve scale throughout Latin America outside of just the home country. At the same time, Latin American companies have also demonstrated the ability to scale outside of Latin America into other countries around the world, which reveals that the culture, while able to keep out foreign competitors, is still capable of being applied outside of Latin America.

In this regard, the cultural friction is one of the biggest success factors for these Latin American companies in achieving uninterrupted scale, coupled with the cultural similarities among the countries throughout the region.

* * *

Governments in Latin America are not just pro-business.

They are pro-venture capital and pro-startup.

Governments in Chile and Mexico have been able to support local venture capitalists by creating subsidized investments as well as more facilitated vehicles in which the investors can invest. As the liberation from investment "rules" starts to emerge and the region starts to become less encumbered by previous government restrictions, the investors in foreign countries that have enjoyed this type of investment freedom in the developed world will begin to flock to Latin America.

Similarly, government-funded accelerators have begun to pop up all over Latin America in order to quickly promote startup growth and increase overall investment at a much more rapid rate than in other markets.

Likewise, the venture capitalists, who have had the previous and crucial operating experience, have begun to realize the importance of "getting their hands dirty" with the startups and undertaking more abnormal measures to help further their portfolio companies.

Such a hands-on approach is not new to investors in Silicon Valley, as that method is partly how venture capitalists in Northern California have been able to generate such great exits—because they know how to operate companies and can advise and act as such.

The Latin American venture capitalists are now beginning to do just that, foreshadowing robust and innovative companies in future years.

The combination of these two ideas of government and investor support allows Latin American startups to more quickly get off the ground and scale, which is a big reason why the region will certainly be "next" and outpace other regional contenders.

* * *

Latin America, at the present moment, is certainly risky from an investor's point of view because the ecosystem is still young.

Nevertheless, the risks that define Latin America—lower potential returns, economic problems of developing countries, smaller exit markets, etc.—are simply due to the fact that the ecosystem is small. And local investors are realizing that and altering short-term strategies accordingly.

Because the investors are able to alter strategies while the ecosystem is developing, such adjustments are what will eventually allow the ecosystem to develop—and the risks stated above will disappear.

At the same time, it is important to understand how not to invest, such as what industries to avoid and how to navigate the region. We will find out later in the book why industries such as social media and national defense are a "no-go" at the present moment and how else not to get burned in the region. That we can identify such industries and risks is a testament to the idea that investing in Latin America is not as difficult as it may seem—because we actually can identify what not to do.

* * *

The rest of this book will delve into much further detail about all the claims made previously and really prove why Latin America scores a perfect eight out of eight.

PART 2

PART 2

CHAPTER 5

INSTITUTIONAL NEED

I have always heard, Sancho, that doing good to base fellows is like throwing water into the sea.

—MIGUEL DE CERVANTES, *EL INGENIOSO HIDALGO DON QUIXOTE DE LA MANCHA*

* * *

In March of 2018, the startup Nubank raised a massive $150 million venture round. With that round, the company has raised a total of $330 million in addition to a $137 million line of credit from Goldman Sachs.[63]

---

63   Penn, David. "Nubank Challenges Brazil's Big Banks in Wake of $150 Million Funding Round." Finovate. March 30, 2018. Accessed August 20, 2018. https://finovate.com/

Is NuBank a product of the New York City, London or Singapore emerging Fintech ecosystems?

No.

NuBank is a Brazilian startup that was founded in 2013 and has grown through an innovative approach to banking many of the un-banked in Brazil.

"In a little less than four years, more than 13 million Brazilians have applied to become a Nubank customer, a reflection of how ready consumers were to welcome new alternatives to the significantly concentrated Brazilian banking market," Nubank founder and CEO David Velez said. "We look forward to expanding our reach and product offering to many millions more in the years ahead."[64]

Nubank's success came as it was able to beat what experts and the company itself has claimed is an unfair business environment where the five biggest Brazilian banks hold 85 percent of assets in the country's highly concentrated banking system.

* * *

---

nubank-challenges-brazils-big-banks-in-wake-of-150-million-in-funding-round/.

64 Ibid.

In Latin America, 49% of the adult population does not have access to a bank account; half of the region is excluded from the formal financial system.[65]

In 2016, Latin America had 450 million smartphones with an estimated 76% of the population expected to own one by the end of 2019.[66]

Couple those two statistics with the fact that in 2016, Latin America also became the region with the largest increase in digital bank accounts, and you have the perfect recipe for an impeccable FinTech boom.

The heart of venture capital in Latin America is FinTech. For international venture capital firms, this industry is typically the first investment they make to get their feet wet before expanding their Latin American portfolios.

"In Latin America, financial services are just ripe for disruption. The banks in these countries are simply not offering good products, and they can get away with it. So these

---

65 Hodgson, Camilla. "The World's 2 Billion Unbanked, in 6 Charts." Business Insider. August 30, 2017. Accessed March 20, 2018. https://www.businessinsider.com/the-worlds-unbanked-population-in-6-charts-2017-8.

66 *The Mobile Economy: Latin America and the Caribbean 2017.* GSMA Intelligence. GSMA Intelligence. 2017. Accessed March 20, 2018. https://www.gsmaintelligence.com/research/?file=e14ff2512ee244415366a89471bcd3e1&download.

startups are already inherently built with the DNA to serve a customer pain point," says Christine Kenna, a partner at Mexico City-based IGNIA Partners.

* * *

If we take a look at the sheer impact of FinTech in the region, the need for these technological advances becomes even more meaningful. At Village Capital, a Washington, D.C.-based venture capital firm with offices in Mexico City, San Francisco, Nairobi, and Bangalore, Rafael Hernández leads the Latin American FinTech team and spoke about his understanding of FinTech companies and their significance to the people of Latin America. As an impact investing-based firm, he and his team always ask a pitching company, "What kind of impact are you having on your community?"

Hernández posed this question to a company called ePesos, a peer-to-peer lending platform, and their response, he says, epitomized the magnitude of the industry in Latin America. In Mexico, the formal banks charge a very high interest rate, yet have no incentive to lower rates because they are still relatively profitable. Due to the high interest rates, ordinary people have difficulty obtaining loans that they will be able to pay back. Companies like ePesos come in and offer a platform for people to obtain loans at much lower interest rates, which allows them to further develop their businesses and other aspects of the economy.

Hernández realized that the "trickle down" effect of these lower interest rates actually allows for national progress.

Hernández asked ePesos, "So if you are still charging interest in the first place, how does this have an impact?" Oscar Robles, the founder of ePesos, responded, "If we do not lend money this way to poor people, they will find illegal forms of obtaining money."

In a place like Mexico, this money could easily come from sources like narco-trafficking or the illegal selling of weapons. By mitigating the need for illegal money, companies like ePesos are reducing the demand for the illegal organizations providing the money and the legal financial institutions that are ripping off the citizens of Latin America.

* * *

"If you look at banks in Latin America, they are incredibly profitable but charge incredibly high prices to consumers, tend to have very poor customer experiences, and tend to be way behind on digital. So all of the things FinTech is trying to accomplish represent these shortcomings in the formal banking system. The gap between a really good FinTech and a bank in Latin America is much larger than anywhere else, which is why this industry is such a hot topic there right now." Bill Cilluffo of QED Investors in Washington, D.C. manages the FinTech-focused venture capital firm's Latin American investments and believes the region is primed for massive returns in this space.

The big hype in Latin American FinTech these days is a company called Nubank. Founded by David Vélez, a former partner at Sequoia, the Brazilian company is the leading provider of digital financial services in the country. Nubank has raised over $617 million, as of October 2018, from prominent firms like Sequoia, Founders Fund, Redpoint, and of course, QED.[67]

In fact, Nubank is Founders Fund's first and only Latin American investment— "a geographic anomaly for Founders Fund," says partner Trae Stephens, showing the magnitude of Nubank's potential.

"They have been in the market for only three and a half years and are approaching three and a half million customers for

---

67 Shieber, Jonathan. "Nubank Is Now worth $4 Billion after Tencent's $180 Million Investment." TechCrunch. October 08, 2018. Accessed October 14, 2018. https://techcrunch.com/2018/10/08/tencent-cash-values-nubank-at-4-billion/.

their credit card products, which is probably faster than any credit card business anywhere has ever grown," says Cilluffo.

One of the main pain points of formal banks that Cilluffo mentioned earlier is the unsatisfactory customer experience, and as he and his team at QED began to evaluate a potential investment in Nubank, they realized that the company completely reversed that plight for consumers.

In looking at Nubank's net promoter score (NPS), which basically asks how likely you are to recommend this product to friends and family and is a good proxy for a user's general passion for the product, Cilluffo found that Nubank had an "almost mathematically impossible" score of 89. To put this score into perspective, a good United States bank would have a net promoter score of around 20. American Express, which is widely regarded to have the best net promoter score in the United States, has a score of around 40, and a really good FinTech's score would be around 60, according to Cilluffo.

Cilluffo and QED realized that because the digitization of financial services is so novel in a country like Brazil, companies like Nubank are likely to have a much better net promoter score than companies in the United States, because for these citizens, their comparative service is exponentially worse.

At the same time, to give Nubank its due credit, the company clearly has a strong formula, which is a testament to its astronomical growth and great potential, given its strong funding rounds.

Cilluffo claims, "What they have done in Latin America is way better than what anyone has done in the United States, just looking back at our time at Capital One and our experiences investing in FinTech companies around the world." One of the main reasons why QED and Nubank decided to engage in this partnership is because David Vélez was partly inspired by the story of Capital One and its revolutionizing of digital finance, as the partners at QED helped found the Capital One. As a result, Cilluffo and QED help advise them on what worked with Capital One and how to bring that technology to Brazil. Simultaneously, Vélez's experience at Sequoia has allowed him to take the "latest and greatest" technology from Silicon Valley and innovate it to bring these resources to a region where they are needed.

Nubank is so innovative that Cilluffo says, "It is much more likely that people here [in the United States] will get inspired and copy what they have done down there."

*　*　*

Similar to David Vélez, Esteban Velasco of Velum Ventures in Colombia has identical goals of moving from the venture capitalist role into running his own FinTech, Sempli.

Through his experiences at Velum and seeing the rise of FinTech, Velasco figured that instead of simply investing in FinTech companies, why not just build off of the successes and failures of his portfolio companies and build his own online lending platform targeting small businesses.

The moment came to him toward the beginning of his first fund as a result of both Velum's investing strategy and the pipeline. Early on, Velasco set out to target a number of verticals in his potential investments, one of which included B2B lending. However, as he began to evaluate some of these platforms for potential capital raise, he did not find any that had suitable operations in which to invest.

In a sense, he figured he could just go out and do it himself.

The final conclusion to start Sempli came after "listening to the market," Velasco says. When he first started Velum, he realized that since the venture capital ecosystem was so young, the entrepreneurs in the region did not really have a sense of what venture capital money was; they did not understand the concept of giving up equity for cash. One-third of his initial deal flow, or at least the companies that were coming to him, were not interested in "smart money." They did not want someone from Velum to be on their board. They did not want a four-to-five-year exit. They wanted loans.

In 2016, after two years of constantly listening to these small and upcoming businesses asking for loans rather than venture capital funding, Velasco finally realized that the market needed a better way for B2B loans but did not have it yet. That is when he decided to start Sempli and knew that it would work. Interestingly, as of 2018, he was managing more money through Sempli than at Velum. As a result, he was stuck with the lingering question whether to go out and try to raise a second fund after two to three years like most venture capital firms, or to commit to Sempli. As you can tell, he chose the latter.

From his experience in managing FinTech portfolio companies and his time at Sempli, Velasco outlines three reasons why these types of platforms trump traditional banks for obtaining loans.

The first is simply that the system is essentially programmed against the people. The majority of smaller companies in Colombia do not have access to traditional credit lines because of the scoring system. "The scoring system, as I have seen, is built around the big businesses," says Velasco. Banks in Colombia typically will not lend without some type of collateral or warranty, which normally are things that small businesses cannot offer. It all boils down to the strategy of traditional banking and the banks' unwillingness to change. "The banks would rather consolidate one million dollars into one company rather than one hundred thousand given to ten different companies," Velasco claims.

The second reason is time. For small businesses the process of obtaining a loan takes around six to eight weeks to even get an answer! Even after receiving an appointment, the bank will say no fifty percent of the time. Of those that do get an offer, Velasco has seen that due to the unreasonably lengthy process, by the time the bank comes around to formally offering a loan, the entrepreneur has no more need for the loan because he or she has already gone to friends and family for the money. As a result of financing through individuals, these small businesses end up paying higher interest rates. With a platform like Sempli, such an approval process takes a mere two or three days, and the businesses do not have to pay such high rates.

The last pain point that lending platforms serve to alleviate is the matter of past experiences. "Small businesses do not like banks." This aversion condenses into the idea that in past negotiations, entrepreneurs have had poor and complicated experiences with these larger banks. The banks in Latin America will say no around fifty percent of the time.

"So how do you possibly come back from that experience?" Velasco says.

* * *

The fact of the matter is that people and small businesses ultimately get discouraged by their experiences with banks but in the past have had no other outlets. Lending platforms like Sempli or ePesos and other FinTech services basically come to the rescue, and that is why FinTech is so popular and thriving in this region.

What is interesting about Sempli and Nubank, however, is that both of these companies were started by ex-venture capitalists. The traditional venture capitalist route is simple: you start a company, you exit, and then you take your operating experience to a venture capital firm. Think Peter Thiel with PayPal, Marc Andreessen with Netscape, or Vinod Khosla with Sun Microsystems. The key here is that all these famous investors went from operator to venture capitalist.

Esteban Velasco and David Vélez are turning the corner and going from venture capitalist to operator. Why? Because the allure of FinTech in Latin America is so much more enticing than the allure of a board seat on the next WhatsApp. "I decided to strike on my own because I had always wanted to be an entrepreneur, and as a venture investor I saw more interesting opportunities on the entrepreneur's side of the table, than in the investor's side of the table," says Vélez.[68]

The journeys and career paths of both Esteban Velasco and David Vélez reveal the sheer power and potential of FinTech—the core of the current Latin American startup boom.

* * *

You would think that the popularity of delivery services here in the United States would not transfer to an emerging market like Latin America, where the infrastructure is quite poor, but such popularity does in fact exist. At first thought, it really does not make sense for businesses in Latin America to provide value based on the use of transportation with individual vehicles.

As I will mention in the next chapter, the culture in Latin America is to travel in buses, which is why many investors see value in bus ticket startups. While Uber and Postmates are popular in the United States due to the convenience factor coupled with the simple technological interface, these types

---

68 Lunden, Ingrid. "Finance Startup Nubank Nabs $14.3M In Sequoia's First Brazil Investment." TechCrunch. September 25, 2014. Accessed March 20, 2018. https://techcrunch.com/2014/09/25/finance-startup-nubank-nabs-14-3m-in-sequoias-first-brazil-investment/.

of services are also on the rise in Latin America for a bit of a different reason.

The Latin American country that has the most cars per one thousand people is Argentina with 314. For reference, countries like the United States, Iceland, and Italy have 795, 745, and 679 cars, respectively, per thousand people. Out of a ranking of 192 countries, Argentina ranks 58th.[69] To put such a figure in perspective, this ranking puts Argentina below countries like Cyprus, Mauritius, and Brunei. For the rest of Latin America, the average ranking in this list sits at 105th. So as you can see, cars are not a particularly popular purchase in Latin America.

So why are vehicle-based startups continuing to emerge in the region?

* * *

Brian York, founder of Bassin Ventures, has actually created a startup himself in Bogotá called Liftit that offers last-mile cargo delivery for businesses in Colombia.

---

69 "Motor Vehicles (per 1,000 People)." Motor Vehicles (per 1,000 People) | Data | Table. 2018. Accessed March 20, 2018. https://web.archive.org/web/20140209114811/http://data.worldbank.org/indicator/IS.VEH.NVEH.P3.

York was born in Colombia but was adopted as a baby and grew up in the United States. He says, "I always wanted to come back and get in touch with my roots. Part of my personal mission in coming back was to help the ecosystem." Nevertheless, before returning to his native country, he spent some time in Silicon Valley as a serial entrepreneur with his own seed fund on the side as well.

When speaking about his decision to start Liftit with two other partners, he mentions, "With my past startups, I had some behind the scenes know-how on go-to-market strategy and understanding what worked and what didn't. So that combined with it really being obvious of the large amount of trucks that are on the road here, we thought that there could be something."

When they first came to Bogotá to test the idea, he posted a singular advertisement picture on Facebook of his partners hoisting a couch onto a truck and promoted it for around five dollars a day and saw requests flood in almost immediately after. "We were pretty overwhelmed with the amount of requests, but we wanted to satisfy the demand, so we essentially ran out into the streets to recruit a driver, hopped in the truck with them, and for the first month and a half to two months, we did every delivery ourselves," he chuckles. The demand for Liftit's services just continued to increase day-by-day as more and more people referred the service to friends and family, and more people heard about them.

York has learned three main lessons from his early start with Liftit as to why his service of last-mile cargo delivery is so valuable to Colombian businesses.

The first value driver is the transparency through technology: understanding where the truck is on the route and who the driver is. Sounds pretty similar to an Uber or Lyft's value proposition, right? Correct—so nothing too different so far.

However, the second takeaway is the on-demand aspect. Big companies in Colombia already have negotiated contracts with established suppliers, but the value of the on-demand cargo delivery really comes from the smaller businesses that not only are unable to negotiate with traditional distributors but also have supply chains that are not as well coordinated and logistically thought out and are constantly changing, unlike the bigger businesses in the region. The smaller players in this market are a main source of value in York's company.

"The last and most important reason but not as obvious to us on day one is that because we are a tech-first company, as we scale up in the business, we drastically reduce cargo costs due to the fact that we are not a traditional transportation company that has a ton of overhead," he says. Liftit can reduce cargo costs by up to 40% as the company scales, trickling down these cost benefits to the consumers, unlike traditional distributors and transportation companies.

But diving deeper, we can see a more general justification as to why delivery services of all kinds are booming in Latin America.

In asking York if he encountered any problems with infrastructure, he assertively replied, "Nope!" And naturally, I was very much expecting the opposite answer, but he continued on to say, "Well, don't get me wrong—the roads are definitely bad and the quality is a problem, but this actually works in our favor."

While the roads are still quite choppy, they are getting better, and in York's experience, as the government continues to help develop infrastructure, it is the businesses that are taking advantage of this trend rather than the consumers. In other words, the entire population of Colombia is not all going to go out and spend thousands of pesos on a car just because the roads are *improving* and not improved; the streets are still pretty rugged. Rather, the businesses and delivery services like Liftit that can adapt to the slightest improvement in infrastructure and find a way to get goods to consumers in a relatively timely manner in some form or another are the ones that investors and the community find the most valuable.

* * *

Perhaps the most popular Latin American delivery service among American investors, which has corralled funding from firms like Sequoia and Andreessen Horowitz, is another Colombian company called Rappi.

Initially, Rappi set out to simply deliver meals and groceries, but co-founder and CEO Simon Borrero realized this delivery concept could grow to something beyond just food delivery.

The moment came to him when he saw that customers started using Rappi's services to have their income tax payments delivered to the local banks. In other words, besides just consumer staple goods, the people in Colombia trusted delivery drivers with thousands of dollars and important tax documents to be given to the bank. Customers even use the application for cash withdrawal by paying for the amount they wanted with credit cards through the app and having the delivery person hand them cash.[70]

---

70 Kokalitcheva, Kia. "Colombian Startup Rappi Wants to Deliver 'Everything'." Fortune. November 8, 2016. Accessed March 20, 2018. http://fortune.com/2016/11/08/rappi-delivery-latin-american/.

The reason behind this, Borrero says, is that ATMs in Colombia are not very safe to use, especially at night. He also mentions that cash withdrawals make up 5% of the company's sales volume.[71] This type of literal financial asset delivery would never even come close to being spoken about as an idea in the United States.

The reason why Rappi generates such high demand for delivery of atypical products in comparison to what delivery services in the developed world offer is that there are fundamental hindrances that prevent citizens from executing simple transactions like ATM withdrawals or driving to a bank and just generally being autonomous in their everyday errands. Rappi, like FinTech, comes to the rescue and serves this function.

Like I mentioned earlier, these kinds of delivery services in the United States are popular because of convenience and straightforward user interface through the use of technology. In Latin America, these kinds of startups are so popular because they satisfy a genuine, deep-rooted issue and need and not a just a luxury. "The on-demand economy, is actually meant to be in emerging markets," claims Borrero.[72] And it will be for the foreseeable future.

---

71 Ibid.
72 Ibid.

* * *

In Latin America and many other emerging economies, many venture capital investments can be classified as impact investments. Venture capitalists that provide capital to companies that have a social mission or seek to provide some sort of overall community benefit while seeking a financial return are making what is known as an impact investment.

Many firms in Latin America have funds strictly dedicated to impact investing, but people may also contend that any investment in a developing economy like Latin America can be labeled as impact.

The most stereotypical view of an impact investment is a company that, in some form, helps people get out of poverty or generally reduces socioeconomic inequality within the region. Yet many people like Nathan Lustig of Magma Partners in Chile categorize impact investments as any that are "creating jobs, training employees, and seeding the next generation of entrepreneurs, while not creating an extractive business model."[73]

---

73 Price, Dennis. "In Latin America, What's an Impact Investment?" ImpactAlpha. February 10, 2018. Accessed March 20, 2018. https://impactalpha.com/in-latin-america-whats-an-impact-investment-9097cd4aec4d/.

Impact investing is so prominent in Latin America that "it is considered a completely different asset class," according to Christine Kenna of IGNIA Partners. The main problem she sees is that impact investing is too vaguely defined and that pretty much everything nowadays is becoming bucketed into impact investing; she thinks "the whole idea of impact investing is overhyped" and wants to boil it down to more specific terms. The main issue is that the majority of the market in Latin America is underserved, so people automatically label anything and everything as impact.

Throughout her time at IGNIA, people classified pretty much everything they invested in as an impact investment.

But that is not what she saw.

On the other hand, she says, "at the end of the day venture capitalists anywhere are looking for the best businesses and the ones that will return the fund." From a venture capitalist's point of view, the focus needs to remain with companies that can produce market returns and stay disciplined in building extremely competitive and compelling products to be sustainable in the long-term.

Despite this ambiguity, there is large opportunity for companies to be successful and profitable by targeting these underserved areas.

The question of what people designate as impact is disputed, but let's dive into some examples of impact investments that we do not and most likely will never see in the United States.

Here is a company in which Kenna and IGNIA invested that leaves zero doubt about its status as an impact investment—this is what she believes is a tried and true company that properly deserves the title. Mexvi is a company focused on building houses for the poorest segments of the Mexican population. When they were investing, the firm realized that such a technology and concept was especially relevant to that community due to the recent earthquakes that struck the country in September of 2017 and February of 2018.

After the earthquakes, houses needed to be rebuilt and "Mexvi is a company that has the ability to quickly and cheaply build high-quality homes for these communities," says Kenna. With an average home costing around $6,000 to build, Mexvi can build one in a matter of weeks. The inherent value of the company does not lie in some super-human ability to build houses; it lies in the partnerships with financial institutions and facilitation of the technical requirements that the company utilizes to provide micro-financing to these families. Kenna mentions, "to the families that use the service, $6,000 is an astronomical amount compared to their life savings, which can be anywhere as small as $250."

Something of this nature is unheard of in the United States and is an example of how venture capitalists get their hands a bit dirtier in the process of investing.

* * *

While looking into potential investments in Mexico, Bill Cilluffo and his team at QED Investors saw that in Mexico, the dominant players within the convenience store market are OXXO and 7-Eleven. Nevertheless, they realized that the market for smaller, independent mom-and-pop stores is arguably even larger, with roughly one million of these shops present. "Just to picture what they look like, think of these bodegas as stores approximately 20% the size of a 7-Eleven, the owners probably living upstairs, and a store downstairs that sells milk, beer, food, and various everyday goods," Cilluffo says.

He mentions that in analyzing the market, "the plethora of these stores makes so much sense, given both the entrepreneurial nature of citizens in an emerging economy like Mexico and its abundance of rural areas and communities." These stores are not just exclusive to Mexico; they are all over Latin America as well.

In comes one of the firm's most recent investments in Latin America—Tienda Pago. The company carries out supply chain financing for corner stores, known as "bodegas" or "tiendas." Tienda Pago partners with milk distributors, beer distributors, etc. and provides very small, weeklong loans to the bodegas in order to finance the inventory purchases. For example, the company will provide a $300 one-week loan to finance the amount of beer that one of these stores would sell in a week. In the United States, stores of this size are nonexistent, and a loan this small would not have any use to businesses of any kind.

In essence, there is a stream of funding at the bottom of the pyramid: the bodegas need a company like Tienda Pago to run their business, and Tienda Pago needs a venture capital company like QED to achieve scale. In order for people in underdeveloped areas to make a living, they need companies like Tienda Pago to provide these micro-loans. In order for Tienda Pago to survive, they need venture capitalists. An investment like this is more of an indirect impact investment, but nonetheless, Cilluffo and his team found a very specific obstacle pertaining to emerging markets and invested in a company that solves this issue.

Especially with the rise of FinTech in Latin America, Cilluffo and QED could have allocated their investment to a less niche business, but instead, they sought to make an impact with this investment and, in his words, "solve a problem that does not need solving in the United States."

Venture capitalists first and foremost are focused on returns and not just on companies that provide for the social good. At the end of the day, a venture capitalist is simply just a professional money manager, whose job is generating returns.

What is so attractive about impact investing and companies like Tienda Pago and Mexvi is not only that are these companies so niche that there is not a flood of venture capitalists fighting with and diluting each other but also that there is a sure-fire, institutional need for these services. Christine Kenna mentions, "The majority of the population in Latin America is moving to what we call 'the emerging middle class,' so we are seeing that you can make enormous businesses with enormous scale if you find the right business model to serve most appropriately this sector of the population."

She goes on to say, "Silicon Valley venture investing and Latin American venture investing are night and day." The consensus is that in Latin America, investments are riskier due to the underdeveloped economy—sure, that makes sense.

I would contend, however, that investments like the ones mentioned above are less risky!

In Silicon Valley, everyone is trying to create some new technology that disrupts established institutions—Uber with taxis, Airbnb with hotels, etc. In Latin America, these impact investments serve a need not yet institutionalized. In other words, these investments are less of a gamble because investors know that there is a market and a need; it is not just a bet on the adoption of the technology. Yes, there is a much lower chance of a company becoming a unicorn, and absolute returns are nowhere close to those that can be generated out of Silicon Valley, but impact investors have a lot less downside risk. The returns might be less, but they are more plausibly forecasted with the chance of going to zero much lower.

* * *

What drives all of these industries mentioned above is not the idea of a billion-dollar exit but rather the fact that there is a very large target market from the onset. Since entrepreneurs and tech companies are beginning to forge the pathway of serving innate and structural needs of the region's consumers, this development allows the ecosystem to mature and lead into the candy technology startups we see in the United States.

Because the fundamental markets are starting to become revolutionized by technology, the mass market can later develop into the disruptive technologies of Silicon Valley. As the basic industries themselves begin to evolve through the use of technology, so will the secondary and complementary industries that drive the substantial, mass adoption and exits we see today in the developed world.

CHAPTER 6

DEFENSIBLE INDUSTRIES

Chi Chi Chi! Le Le Le! We are the miners of Chile!
—THE 34 CHILEAN MINERS AS THEY
WERE BEING RESCUED IN 2010

* * *

When I was 13 years old, I participated in a two-week immersion trip to Costa Rica through a school program. During the trip, our group of 25 seventh graders plus two faculty sponsors spent a week in the mountainous and rainforest-filled city of Monteverde as well as a week in the polar opposite beach town of Flamingo.

Our experience in Monteverde was filled with zip-lining, rainforest hikes, and observing various wildlife in what the locals call the "cloud forest" city, which sits over 4,600 feet above sea level.

One of our excursions in the cloud forest included a visit to a Costa Rican *finca*, which translates to a farm. The produce and livestock we saw at the farm included spinach, tomatoes, radishes, and chicken. We even had a meal at the farm, which was all sourced directly from the ground on which we walked!

As we toured the thirty-acre farm, we saw workers laboring and excavating the crops to sell in the local market as well as to the local grocery stores. Our guide mentioned that one of the reasons why many farmers still lived in poverty in Costa Rica was because they simply do not have the capacity to produce enough volume to sell to the distributors and retailers.

In the United States, technology in the agricultural sector was prevalent and farmers had developed efficient processes and techniques for growing and cultivating crops, whereas in Costa Rica, much of the tedious harvesting was still done by hand. He mentioned that if there were quicker and more productive ways of farming, then this industry that was so essential to the national economy would achieve better scale more quickly.

My visit to that farm was over eight years ago in 2010. It is now 2018. I guess somewhere out there, the agriculture gods listened to this farmer's plea for innovation, as "agritech" (agriculture technology) is an industry that is revolutionizing such a staple sector in Latin America and one where investors see large potential for success.

* * *

While the industries mentioned in the previous chapter illustrate examples of how technological startups in the region are serving the basic needs of citizens, emerging markets still need industries that have some sort of resistance against foreign startups that could have the capacity to out-scale local companies. In other words, emerging markets need to have certain industries that really are proprietary to the region itself and have the potential to become evolved through technology.

Latin America is exhibiting just that—through its own "niche" industries and clones.

* * *

Juliane Butty of Seedstars visited Chile to explore the country's startup scene and truly witnessed why the media call it "Chilecon Valley." Chile is known to be the innovation center of Latin America; innovative startups in all different kinds of interesting industries like biotech, cleantech, and mining have been popping up in the country. At the same time, the agritech industry has been a popular source of value for investors, and while still in its early stages, the sector is primed for rapid growth.

"Some of these startups in agritech are basically scientific," mentions Butty. During her visit, she analyzed a Santiago-based company called The Not Company. The company analyzes DNA in plants and translates this plant DNA into recreating foods like meat, cheese, and milk without the need to harvest livestock. The company basically utilizes a computer program called "Giuseppe," which is an artificial intelligence algorithm that recreates food formulas to replicate taste and texture for desired foods traditionally based on animal inputs.

When she was speaking with the founders and exploring the business, Butty realized that what they do for farmers is actually complementary rather than substitutive. While recreating these animal products may seem like removing the need for farmers, the farmers still need to grow and cultivate these plants for the DNA analysis. By growing these plants and replicating these types of foods, farmers do not have to wait so long for livestock to produce these inputs and can therefore sell products more efficiently, helping alleviate the plight of the farmer I met eight years ago.

I see the future of these cultural food companies as partnering with the farmers rather than eliminating them.

Recently, The Not Company raised capital from a venture capital firm in Chile. "It is a sector where we see venture capitalists and accelerators raising funds and programs just for these types of businesses. Not only does it show high growth, but it also is a sector that has a huge impact on the whole population," declares Butty.

Agriculture is such an important sector to the Latin American economy because traditionally, countries in Latin America have been the largest exporters of soybeans, cacao, coffee, chicken, and many other products due to the fertile lands of the region. "If [the region] wants to keep growing, they need to find innovative ways of maintaining production but at the same time doing so in a sustainable way, without using up all of the natural resources. Such growth and sustainability needs technology," asserts Butty. When she visited The Not Company and saw that the company both helps farmers scale their operations as well as does so in a sustainable manner, that was the moment she realized that the company had a bright future.

Additionally, Butty visited Nxtp.Labs, an accelerator in Chile, which launched the first agritech-only accelerator program in mid-2016.[74] Butty witnessed two companies that do not necessarily operate in the same way as The Not Company but are more focused on the "efficient farming" aspect of agritech in which we can see more direct, reciprocal effects for farmers.

* * *

Sao Paulo-based BovControl is currently a company in the portfolio at Nxtp.Labs, and the startup focuses on helping farmers maximize meat production through what the founder, Danilo Leao, calls "the internet of cows." Leao began taking care of his family's land at just 15 years old, where he manually tracked livestock with a spreadsheet and traditional ear tags. While this was standard procedure, he wanted to find a way to speed up the production for meat and dairy farmers.[75]

---

74 Burwood-Taylor, Louisa. "NXTP Labs Launches First Latin American Agtech Accelerator." AgFunderNews. July 17, 2016. Accessed March 21, 2018. https://agfundernews.com/nxtp-labs-launches-first-ever-agtech-accelerator-latin-america.html/.

75 Schwartz, Ariel. "The 'Internet of Cows' Is Taking over Farms across the World." Business Insider. January 24, 2017. Accessed March 21, 2018. https://www.businessinsider.com/bovcontrol-internet-of-cows-2017-1.

BovControl allows farmers to input a cow's data, such as birthdate, vaccination history, and weight, and with a Bluetooth-enabled collar, the application can track a cow's location and make predictions for when a cow may give birth if she is pregnant and when the optimal time is for slaughter. Push notifications also allow for less micro-managing and updates the farmer daily on the status of each cow.

A local farmer named Bruno manages an 830-cow farm and mentioned, "I used pen and paper before. I do a lot of vaccinations, and the app gives me tools to collect that data and keep track of expiration dates. When a cow gives birth, I can capture the animal's growth and figure out when I should sell it. It completely changes the way I do my job."[76] As of October 2018, the company has received over $1.2 million in funding.[77]

Additionally, another Nxtp.Labs company, Kilimo, provides analytics tools for irrigation management and helps farmers determine the optimal irrigation prescription for each crop. Founder Jairo Trad claims that the application "improves yields by over 30% and water use efficiency by up to 70%."[78]

---

76 Ibid.
77 BovControl: Funding Rounds." Crunchbase. Accessed October 14, 2018. https://www.crunchbase.com/organization/bovcontrol#section-funding-rounds
78 "Kilimo - More Yields with Less Water." Kilimo - More Yields with Less Water. Accessed March 20, 2018. http://www.kilimo.com.ar/.

But why do such technologies like BovControl and Kilimo deserve venture funding? What value do they bring?

Many people in Latin America still live in poverty and do not have access to food, so during her visit to Chile, Butty realized there still needs to be improvements in the supply and quantity of food. In the United States, such a problem does not exist. "Improved irrigation helps solve the problem of people being hungry in Latin America, something that does not exist in developed markets," says Butty. The applications, which are farmer-friendly and focus on economical farming, help everyone down the supply chain and allow farmers to scale more quickly.

"Agritech is set to be the most popular sector in Argentina, Chile, and Brazil, next to FinTech," says Esteban Campero, Undersecretary of Entrepreneurs at Argentina's Ministry of Production.[79]

* * *

In addition to agritech, startups helping innovate the mining sector are proving fruitful. Mining represents over 55% of the

---

79 Kendall, Matt. "Argentina Startups Aim at the Agritech Boom ." Nearshore Americas. April 19, 2017. Accessed March 21, 2018. https://www.nearshoreamericas.com/argentina-startups-aim-at-the-agritech-boom/.

exports of Chile[80]—the country's economy depends on this sector. But like agriculture, mineral resources are limited and even more so, run a bigger risk of depletion. Because Chile is so highly reliant on the mining industry, innovative companies are beginning to appear and deliver value to investors and mining companies. "If you can find the gap for value to be delivered in mining, then of course, you will have clients," mentions Andres Araos of Start-Up Chile.

At the accelerator, Araos has witnessed a company called Soji come through the program. The startup offers robots to automatically clean solar panels. This relates to mining, interestingly, because solar panels are used as one of the main providers of energy for mining in Chile. The country's Atacama Desert, in fact, is full of private solar plants that only feed the mining industry.

Fascinatingly, Soji was actually created in the United Kingdom and then moved to Chile to take advantage of Start-Up Chile's accelerator program. Initially, the robots were solely set up to clean windows and rooftops, but the mentors in the accelerator saw that the devices could easily apply to solar panels with a few minor tweaks. In other words, the team at

---

80 Shaw-Smith, Peter. "Chile Continues Dry Bulk Dominance." Chile Continues Dry Bulk Dominance | IHS Fairplay. April 12, 2018. Accessed April 25, 2018. https://fairplay.ihs.com/bulk/article/4299736/chile-continues-dry-bulk-dominance.

Start-Up Chile saw that Soji's product could be used to tap into the lucrative mining industry and produce more value for customers and investors.

When he was analyzing the company, Araos realized that it is not necessarily always essential to innovate as a direct solution to the operations but that complementary companies can contain profound value. "Soji was able to find which part of the value chain they fit into and was able to provide benefits accordingly," mentions Araos. Soji has since graduated from the accelerator program and received multiple funding rounds.

One of the main reasons why innovation in these staple industries provide so much value, especially in Latin America, to not only the general economy but also to venture capitalists, is that in the United States, "entrepreneurs have evolved to be creative and develop new technologies and entertainment like Snapchat and Airbnb, whereas they do not have this mindset in Latin America. There are bigger issues in Latin America that need to be solved first," claims Butty. Developed markets do not have these institutional issues like in Latin America, so the way to find value in developed economies is through creative and disruptive technologies. In Latin America, mining and agriculture are so essential to the economy that investors find value in these sectors, which have previously suffered from a severe lack of modernization.

Araos asserts, "Especially in emerging markets, just look at what are the biggest industries, and that is where you will find the biggest opportunities to innovate." Because agritech and mining have previously been underdeveloped in terms of innovation but at the same time are so crucial to the economies of many of these Latin American countries, there is a lot of opportunity to advance these sectors technologically.

Sectors like these are defensible because they are so particular to the region itself; there is little threat of companies like Soji or BovControl originating in a place like Silicon Valley and scaling to overtake startups in Chile or Argentina. Where there is genuine need is where these technologies will arise. And this need is not in the developed world; it is in the developing world.

* * *

A few years ago, I visited Argentina with my family. Of course, we were in Buenos Aires for most of the trip, but for a few days in the middle we visited Iguazu Falls, the waterfall that forms a three-way border with Argentina, Brazil, and Paraguay. Think of Iguazu as the Niagara Falls of South America but not as touristy and more authentic.

After taking a bumpy flight on a relatively shanty and Ryanair-esque plane, we arrived in the rural city. While the economy of Iguazu thrives basically on tourism, the city was much less developed than I thought. Dirt roads, local corner stores, and a lot of fields epitomized the view for most of the drive to our three-story hotel.

As we planned to stay for a couple days, we hired a driver, whose name was Fernando. Married with two kids, this short and incredibly sweet man became our lifesaver throughout our stay in Iguazu.

Eventually, we had to stop for gas during our adventures, and I noticed something a bit peculiar, yet unsurprising after remembering where I was. Before filling up our mid-sized, white SUV, Fernando went inside the shoddy station to pre-pay for the gas, and having been a driver for most of his career, he knew exactly how much gas he needed and pre-paid an accurate amount.

As he finished pumping the gas, I looked at the pump and noticed that there was no screen of any sort or any way to insert a credit card before filling up. The pump was literally just there for the nozzle.

I initially thought it odd for a gas station to not have a "pay-at-the-pump" mechanism, but I realized that being in such a rural city made me understand the types of technologies and conveniences we take for granted in the developed world.

* * *

At Parallel 18 in Puerto Rico, a company called Gasolina Móvil is experiencing great success after graduation from the government-funded accelerator. As Cyril Meduña, who sits on the advisory board, witnessed the company's development during its time in the accelerator, he knew the company would be poised to revolutionize Latin America.

In Puerto Rico and most of Latin America in general, no pay-at-the-pump technology exists. The issue is that "the gas companies have no desire to use capital on transforming the existing pumps to be digitally enabled to accept credit cards at the pump," says Meduña. Because the gas companies were unwilling to change, the founders of Gasolina Móvil took it upon themselves to find a solution and invented an application that allows people to pay through their phone without the need to go in the store before every fill-up. The app works in such a way that the user just scans the barcode on the pump itself, which allows the app to identify the specific pump and connect it to the right gas station and then processes payments from there.

These talented founders understood the genuine need and proof of concept through seeing the established norm in the United States. Since Gasolina Móvil's departure from Parallel

18, they have partnered with Puma Energy, one of the largest oil and gas distribution companies in Latin America.

The ultimate success behind Gasolina Móvil and what Parallel 18 and Puma saw in the company was the regional need for the technology. Everyone talks about the clone startups popping up in emerging markets like food-delivery services or Uber copy cats, but Gasolina Móvil is what I call an *institutional clone*. The pay-at-the-pump concept already exists in the United States, and the company is not copying another successful startup that introduced such a technology but rather a concept already taken for granted in the United States—hence the institutional denomination. For these types of clones, the proof of concept phase is virtually nonexistent, as they know the technology works; it is just a matter of being able to scale and market.

And why is this defensible? Because there are no "startups," per se, that engage in this type of business in the developed world. Should anyone from the developed world try to implement this technology in an emerging market, it would have to come through the oil and gas companies, which in emerging markets, tend to be local or state-owned. In that regard, Gasolina Móvil really has no threat, especially given that the company has already partnered with a large corporation in the region.

* * *

In mentioning these clone startups in Latin America, let's now dive into an example.

Bus tickets startups are hitting it big.

In the United States, we have the ease of obtaining both cheap tickets and cheap transportation. Think of services like Stubhub, Lyft, and Greyhound Lines.

"In Latin America, we usually travel from one city to another in a bus. Why? Because people are poorer and travel in buses due to the roads and infrastructure having been designed from the start to be used for buses," says Luis Castañeda of Axon Partners Group. As he has been analyzing potential investments for Axon's current and future funds, he sees a strong play in startups that offer online bus ticket services to consumers.

A partner at a prominent venture capital firm in Latin America that wishes to maintain anonymity spoke to me about his investment in Guichê Virtual, a Brazilian startup that does just that. In addition to bus tickets, the company has since expanded to offer online ferry bookings. Founded by Thiago Carvalho, Rodrigo Barbosa, and Halyson Valadão, the company connects passengers to various bus companies throughout Brazil and allows people to purchase bus tickets online without the need to go to the bus station in advance of the trip.

Companies like Guichê Virtual and Grubhub-like, food delivery clones succeed in Latin America because they have a direct case study in the United States to build off of both successes and mistakes when developing their own business model. The main reasons why these startups in the United States do not just expand themselves is because of the cultural barriers within the region and the fact that the startups are probably still not profitable domestically and need to fine-tune their services in the United States first. After seeing the concept and the technology, startups in Latin America pop up and copy because concepts like online ticketing and food delivery are not proprietary to American society—it is just that Silicon Valley's mature ecosystem embodies a culture of first-movers.

* * *

At the same time, these clones in Latin America arguably understand the formula better; they figure out what went wrong and improve upon it.

At Velum Ventures in Colombia, Esteban Velasco invested in a company called Hogaru, which provides cleaning services to small and medium-sized businesses in Latin America.

When he was evaluating a potential investment in Hogaru, he says, "I looked back at the direct case study with Homejoy in the United States." Homejoy essentially provided the same service of connecting professional cleaners to clients and looked quite promising with over fifty million dollars of funding from investors like Redpoint, Andreessen Horowitz, and First Round Capital.[81] Ultimately, Homejoy went bankrupt due to lawsuits over whether their workers were independent contractors or employees, with the former being what Homejoy sought.[82]

After seeing the initial failure of a similar company in the United States, the outlook for Hogaru did not look optimistic, but Velasco knew that customers would use the service. In the end, he invested in Hogaru and learned from the past mistake of Homejoy by actually hiring the cleaners as employees, and as a result, "Everyone is happy," says Velasco. Currently, Hogaru has over six hundred employees.

---

81 Homejoy: Funding Rounds." Crunchbase. Accessed October 14, 2018. https://www.crunchbase.com/organization/homejoy#section-funding-rounds

82 Madden, Sam. "Why Homejoy Failed ... And The Future Of The On-Demand Economy." TechCrunch. July 31, 2015. Accessed March 21, 2018. https://techcrunch.com/2015/07/31/why-homejoy-failed-and-the-future-of-the-on-demand-economy/.

The cleaning service itself worked for Homejoy, so Velasco knew that there was no technological or product risk with Hogaru and that such a service did not just apply to American consumers—it was just a matter of adjusting the operational strategy. Today, Hogaru currently sits well in Velum's portfolio, and Velasco sees a bright exit ahead.

Venture capitalists like Castañeda, Velasco, and Guichê Virtual's investor utilize the examples from the United States to justify their investments, easing concerns about technological and product risk. While the clones are not necessarily radically innovative, they are alive and well in Latin America with venture capitalists pouncing at these opportunities and making significant returns.

For the most part, these clones survive because of local market knowledge. "There are some business models that are global by nature and that could develop and expand out of San Francisco or Palo Alto, but instead [those that interest us are] those for which local presence is fundamental, that require local teams to execute and local market knowledge," said Nicolás Szekasy of Kaszek Ventures in an interview with PulsoSocial.[83]

---

83 Herrera, Clarisa. "Nicolás Szekasy of Kaszek Ventures on Why Local Know-How Is Key." PulsoSocial. December 20, 2013. Accessed March 21, 2018. https://pulsosocial.com/en/2013/12/20/nicolas-szekasy-of-kaszek-ventures-on-why-local-know-how-is-key/.

While the business model can be applied anywhere, Szekasy and his team look for the companies that can utilize this business model and the local "know-how" to create friction from outsiders and create a more sustained competitive advantage in that way. That is why these Latin American clones survive and are generally more defensible than people may think.

Clones like these are defensible first because there are cultural barriers to these foreign startups in entering the Latin American market, which require some sort of local know-how or twist that the clones inherently already contain; secondly, the clones themselves have the first-mover advantage in their respective regions because they emerge before the original company in the developed world is profitable domestically and therefore is not yet focused on expanding abroad.

* * *

What these industries like agritech and mining-tech as well as these clones have in common is that they emphasize the locality of the sectors and the business operations. This local friction and local need is key to the defensibility of startups that emerge in a developing market and why the Latin American startup environment will not be susceptible to being out-paced or out-scaled by companies in the developed world.

CHAPTER 7

CULTURAL ALLIANCES

Anyone who pretends to "understand" Latin America is a fool.
—MICHAEL HOGAN

* * *

In 2013, a Central American dollar store chain got a big boost.

It was not from a funding round, and it was not from organic expansion.

Dollar City, the Central American company with around fifteen stores at the time, entered into an agreement with Montreal-based Dollarama to receive business expertise and strategic resources for further expansion into Latin America, specifically Ecuador, Colombia, and Peru.

So did Dollar City give up any equity? No. Did Dollar City need any capital commitment? No.

"Our objective is to test the potential of the Latin American market in a way that minimizes risk, capital and time investment and we believe that we have found the right strategic approach and the right partners to achieve this," says Dollarama CEO Larry Rossy.[84]

So why did Dollarama not just expand organically into Latin America?

Because the local expertise of Dollar City facilitates the Latin American learning curve for Dollarama's management. The transaction may seem one-sided in that Dollar City receives the scale and benefits from Dollarama, but in reality, Dollarama gets the local knowledge and steady diffusion of knowledge about the Latin American environment.

---

84 Dollarama. "Dollarama Enters into an Agreement to Provide Business Expertise and Sourcing Services to Central American Dollar Store Chain Dollar City." News release, February 5, 2013. Dollarama. Accessed August 20, 2018. http://www.dollarama.com/wp-content/uploads/2013/02/Barcelona-release_Feb-5-v014-SEDAR.pdf.

Rossy mentions, "This collaboration with Dollar City will provide us with a timely window and a strategic entry point to participate in the long-term potential of this dynamic emerging market. Furthermore, we believe that our product offering can be easily adapted to appeal to local tastes as well as offer consumers tremendous value."[85]

The partnership was just as simple as that—no equity, no capital. All that was transferred was advice and resources. The scale of Dollarama will allow Dollar City to ignite the market and reach consumers even more quickly.

Dollar City's ease and willingness to partner reveals the reality and potential for these alliances across industries in Latin America. And the influx of these partnerships will allow these industries to scale more quickly and efficiently for years to come.

* * *

In mentioning the local friction points that are so essential to keeping foreign startups out and letting Latin American companies scale organically, it may sound like only those who know the landscape and the culture can invest.

---

85   Ibid.

While the vast cultural differences may seem incredibly daunting and are the reason why investors and the media tend to stay away from the region, there are definitely solutions for traversing this trail. If the local startups or companies are willing to partner with foreign companies that want to provide resources or expertise, then both of these players can gain a mutual benefit and that is how an emerging market will become global.

* * *

Arguably the biggest risk venture capitalists see when investing in Latin America is the lack of knowledge of the culture and the social landscape. This obviously makes sense because people's preferences, customs, and habits are always different around the world. Of course, this type of risk persists in any emerging economy, which leaves investors with three choices: invest autonomously, create a strategic or complementary alliance, or refuse to invest altogether. The safest and most competent strategy would be to create a cultural alliance, especially if investing for the first time.

These types of alliances do not just pertain to venture capitalists who are afraid of losing their investment—large corporations have also been partaking in these plays for years. Miguel Monteverde worked for Discovery Communications for nine years and was most recently a senior vice president in their digital media division.

During his time with Discovery, he mentioned that the corporation engaged in a joint venture with NET, a Brazilian company, when launching Discovery Kids in Latin America in 2010. In Brazil, Discovery Kids was instituted as an over-the-top (OTT) streaming service, which can be thought of as a Netflix-type platform, rather than a linear television business—a typical cable channel.

Interestingly, when Monteverde and Discovery launched the new business, the OTT service did not already exist in the United States for two main reasons.

"The challenge that Discovery has in the United States, specifically is that they have an enormously lucrative linear television business that makes the company about three to four billion dollars in revenue annually. Anything that they would do that would cannibalize or eat in to that, like a streaming service, where people would cancel their subscriptions to cable service and not watch the linear television channel, is a very scary proposition," says Monteverde. The introduction of the OTT service in the United States could have caused users of the linear television business to switch to the new platform, thereby leading to a loss of customers through the addition of another product.

The second and less glaring reason was that "in Latin America, they really did not have anything at stake; they could take more chances and more risks." In other words, Discovery Kids was a more experimental venture, as the company did not have any other major business lines to be threatened; there was no need to defend any already lucrative businesses.

They decided to enter the partnership with NET due to the company's knowledge of local content and experience. The Discovery-NET union is known as a strategic, geographic partnership, as the two operate in the same industry but in different markets. "As I have witnessed countless times, companies, especially in the media space, will just repurpose the content from the main market to the foreign market," Monteverde says.

While, by all means, Discovery could have sent employees to the region or hired people to analyze the market, that would have taken months just to obtain an accurate data set. For the sake of saving time and R&D costs, they engaged in a joint venture in order to immediately and accurately deliver content to viewers.

As a result, Discovery Kids became the most viewed kids' programming service in the region.

While this example is not related to venture capital or start-ups, it is important to take away that local businesses in Latin America like NET, especially in the technology and consumer-driven space, will continue to thrive and face less risk of foreign competition because the need for local knowledge of the region is so imperative for success.

In the case of venture capital, rather than trying to expand a portfolio company into Latin America to take advantage of some upcoming consumer trend within the region, it is most likely more worth the time and resources to invest in a local business that is attempting to capture this market.

But how can venture capitalists adequately evaluate the business if they have no knowledge of the region?

* * *

While strategic partnerships can be useful for companies looking to break into foreign markets, complementary partnerships can alternatively be utilized for the same purpose.

In 2016, Bill Cilluffo and QED Investors partnered with Scotiabank to promote FinTech startups in Latin America. Headquartered in Toronto, Canada, Scotiabank is the third largest Canadian bank by market capitalization and deposits but also has around half of its business in Latin America, according to Cilluffo.

The majority of QED's FinTech investments in the past have been in Brazil, so they have come to understand that region very well. Despite this, the firm is still headquartered in Washington, D.C. and does not have ample access to the rest of the Latin American market, so they partnered with a company that has a significant presence in Mexico, Peru, Colombia, and Chile.

Although QED knows Brazil well, that knowledge does not simply translate to the rest of Latin America. Culturally, Brazil is a completely different ballgame. The Brazilian economy is entirely distinct from the rest of the region—consumers have different preferences and businesses operate in different ways. In addition, the country even speaks another language. The fact that QED chose to partner with Scotiabank reveals the sheer volume of cultural hurdles for investors not just in journeying from the United States to Latin America but even as close as from Brazil to Colombia!

As for the idea of the complementary partnership, Cilluffo and his team wanted a partner that not only had a strong presence but also an "ambitious digital transformation agenda." When they set out initially to form the partnership, Cilluffo and his team said, "We made sure to understand how can they fill in some of our weaknesses, and how can we help them understand the FinTech space better." Essentially, the partnership helps QED "get our feet on the ground and helps us get to know some of the ecosystems in ways we could not really do from here."

Scotiabank chose QED to get closer to the FinTech space and create an alliance with a firm that has a broad understanding of building up early-stage FinTech business models. In fact, Scotiabank currently acts as a limited partner in QED's fund as well. "The goal is when we make investments in companies, to see whether or not there are opportunities for them to do commercial partnerships with some of our investments," says Cilluffo. In turn, QED receives not only the funding but also the general experience of regional consumer trends within the financial sector and various strategic resources to further develop these businesses.

* * *

Venture capitalists realize the cultural barriers to investing in Latin America, but the increasing potential of startups in the region is bait they cannot leave hanging. In order to efficiently and quickly capture value from these budding businesses, firms are beginning to partner with regional companies that understand the ecosystem. In turn, these regional players either receive the benefit of a larger company that can provide scalable resources or of a company that can provide new capabilities. Either way, there is a mutual benefit for both the foreign company and the local company.

I am not saying all venture capital firms form these types of partnerships, but many American firms are beginning to see Latin America as a burgeoning region entrepreneurially and want to quickly establish a foothold in this market. In order to effectively do so initially, they are creating these alliances.

Because Latin America has been able to provide these opportunities for complementary and strategic alliances through the examples mentioned above, this notion allows the startups of the region to scale for two main reasons.

The first is that because there is such a cultural gap between the emerging and developed market, it allows for natural defensibility against startups from, say, Silicon Valley. Think about how MercadoLibre has been able grow and create such a presence in the region and how Amazon has lagged behind in the Latin American market.

The second reason is that if the developing market allows for foreign players to partner, then these larger, external companies can provide resources and expertise to these smaller startups that may have difficulty gaining ground due to the young ecosystem.

At the end of the day, success in foreign markets boils down to bridging the cultural gap.

CHAPTER 8

CULTURAL SCALABILITY

You must not judge people by their country. In South America, it is always wise to judge people by their altitude.

— PAUL THEROUX

* * *

At Village Capital, Rafael Hernández spoke about his working with Mutuo Financiera, a lending platform for small businesses. As Hernández began to work with the Mexico-based company in its early stages, he says he knew that, "Mexico was already a pretty large enough addressable market for a company that offers loans to the 93% of businesses that get rejected from the larger banks."

Nevertheless, the issue he saw was not in the business model but in physically finding clients for the company.

After long negotiation with his team, he took Mutuo Financiera, along with a few other portfolio companies, on an all-expenses-paid trip to Colombia for one week. In total, he took five Mexican companies, two Argentinian companies, and two Chilean companies.

While in Colombia, Hernández and Village Capital negotiated meetings with other venture capital firms, potential partners, and institutions for Mutuo Financiera to establish relationships and get a feel for doing business in Colombia. Within this week, "Mutuo Financiera lined up several potential clients and other venture capitalists to partner with," Hernández mentions.

The business model immediately caught on—it really was just a matter of establishing the relationships. In just four months since its inception, the company already had operations in two countries and is continuing to expand.

Companies like Mutuo Financiera have the ability to scale all over Latin America because culturally and economically, these types of business models apply almost anywhere in the region.

In addition, Hernández and his team also took the four companies from Argentina and Chile and added three companies from Colombia to visit Mexico City in the same fashion, and saw similarly successful results.

This is the magnitude of the cultural scalability of Latin America's tech ecosystem.

* * *

But if the culture is so vastly different, how can these startups really and truly grow into the companies we see from Silicon Valley?

In the introduction of this book, I mentioned that the whole of Latin America, rather than just one city, would become the home of the next tech boom. The reason I say this is because of Latin America's facilitated allowance of regional scalability.

* * *

We have heard countless times that startups need to achieve scale, no matter where they come from. In the United States, it is definitely possible for a radically innovative company to quickly achieve scale because certain ventures need only one formula to reach a population of over 327 million people. The size of the population is a main advantage behind American ventures. In Latin America, countries do not have such a high population. Brazil has the largest with over 210 million, but let's exclude Brazil for now because of its cultural separation from the rest of Latin America. Mexico has the next largest population with over 130 million, and Colombia follows with over 49 million.[86]

So from an initial overview, Latin American countries do not have the population advantage as the United States does, but what both venture capitalists and I have witnessed is that a venture implemented in Mexico could easily have been done in Colombia, for example. In other words, the immediate scalability potential of startups in Latin America far exceeds just the home market. In fact, Mexico is not the home market for a startup originating in Mexico; its home market is Latin America.

* * *

As with our chapter on cultural alliances, let's begin with a little teaser from the corporate level.

---

86 "Countries in Latin America and the Caribbean by Population (2018)." Countries in Latin America and the Caribbean by Population (2018) - Worldometers. 2018. Accessed October 14, 2018. http://www.worldometers.info/population/countries-in-latin-america-and-the-caribbean-by-population/.

Imagine a corporation about to launch a new product. How do they do so? Usually they beta test it with a smaller sample size and then roll it out further if it becomes a success with this smaller group.

If we look at what companies like Uber or Amazon have done, the former tested its self-driving taxis in Pittsburgh. Though Uber had some issues with this technology, they have reflected upon these accidents and further corrected those technological shortcomings and resumed testing. Eventually, once the company receives adequate data and feedback, the technology will hopefully be available nationally in a matter of years.

Amazon has been doing the same with its two-hour, Whole Foods delivery test in Austin, Cincinnati, Dallas, and Virginia Beach. The importance of these examples is that these companies simply need to test in only one city to acquire the results they need to roll the new innovation out to 327 million people.

In Latin America, companies like Panasonic, Samsung, and Sony do the same but with a slight twist. As Chile is known to be the innovation hub of Latin America, when these foreign companies test a new electronic product for the Latin American market, they do so in Chile. Should the product perform well, they then roll it out to the rest of Latin America; they know that it will work in the other countries due to the cultural similarities.

In the United States, if it works in Pittsburgh, it will work in Phoenix. In Latin America, if it works in Chile, it will work in Colombia.

* * *

As Bob Dorf, serial entrepreneur and co-author of *The Startup Owners Manual*, set out into mentoring 123Seguro, he thought the advisory journey would be a walk in the park. Reminiscing on the dozens of Latin American startups he had worked with previously, he did not see many roadblocks for the online auto insurance company. With the rise of e-commerce and general Internet access for the majority of Latin America, the two co-founders, Bruno and Martín Ferrari, hopped on the trend with the insurance sector.

When they began in Argentina, they immediately hired a Colombian manager to learn the business model while they initiated the business in the Argentinian market to quickly expand further. The company knew that it made no difference to the adoption of the technology whether they started in Argentina or Colombia, or whether they hired an Argentinian or Colombian manager. Soon after launch, they were in Argentina, Colombia, and Mexico.

Dorf was excited about their technology of automated response systems, as the efficiency of such a model yielded slashed costs for many companies in the United States. Unfortunately, "123Seguro struggled initially in achieving sales, as only four quote requests out of every ten thousand impressions yielded sales," Dorf recalls. He and the two brothers were "flabbergasted." The company easily scaled into the rest of Latin America with no hiccups to the business operations, yet its sales were stagnant. Eventually, Dorf had his eureka moment.

Latin Americans are multi-active. No, that does not mean they are always multi-tasking; it's one of the three cultural categories of the Lewis Model, which buckets countries into three dimensions of behavior—multi-active, linear-active, and reactive. A multi-active culture displays feelings and emotions more outwardly and values interactions with people. A linear-active country, like the United States or Germany, is more jobs and facts-oriented and remains a bit more formal in interaction. Reactive countries, like Japan and China, are more reserved and never reveal feelings outwardly.[87]

Dorf realized, "Latin Americans react more negatively toward automation and value these real-person interactions."

---

87 "The Lewis Model – Dimensions of Behaviour." Cross Culture. June 22, 2015. Accessed March 22, 2018. https://www.crossculture.com/the-lewis-model-dimensions-of-behaviour/.

Immediately, he suggested the company switch to a phone call follow-up when a customer requests a quote. The brothers tested out the method in Argentina and immediately found rapid success. Customers and salespeople could finally build these trust-based relationships that Latin Americans value so highly. After implementing the practice in Mexico and Colombia, their sales problem was virtually solved.

I wish I could tell you it really is that simple, because in the grand scheme of things, venture capitalists are seeing the elemental transferability of these businesses around the region. On the other hand, they find that companies still need to adjust certain aspects of their practices and business model when scaling, as with any business.

Comically, Dorf noted that when they implemented the sales call prompts in Colombia, they noticed a slight discrepancy in sales initially. After some more research he and the brothers realized that while their final hook of "Okay, so do you want me to sign you up or not?" really lassoed in customers in Argentina, "that sort of phrase was considered highly offensive in Colombia," he says. So as a reality check, this trivial story informs us that such regional scaling is not always so straightforward.

It is important to realize, however, that these countries have very similar underlying cultures and preferences. In the case of 123Seguro, if you are hitting it off in one country, you can hit it off in the rest, but if you are missing the mark in one, you are going to miss the mark everywhere else.

As a result of these resemblances, the company has received millions of dollars in outside capital from investors, including a fund from MercadoLibre[88], the poster child of Latin America's regional integration.

To achieve adequate scale and return for investors, these Latin American startups need to operate in countries outside of their country of origin as well. Luckily, the integration capabilities are almost automatic from a business model and cultural point of view.

In the United States, a company only needs one formula to reach a population of 327 million. In Chile, a company only needs one formula to reach not just the country's population of 18 million but also a Latin American population of over 400 million.

* * *

---

88 "Mercado Libre, NXTP Labs & Alaya Capital Invest in 123Seguro." LAVCA | Latin American Private Equity & Venture Capital Association. December 20, 2017. Accessed March 22, 2018. https://lavca.org/2017/12/20/mercado-libre-nxtp-labs-alaya-123seguro/.

I elaborated on the integration potential of startups throughout the rest of Latin America. But venture capitalists, especially those in Silicon Valley, are always looking for the next unicorn.

In this day and age, the increasing interconnectedness of globalization has allowed companies to extend their reach far past their home market. In the startup world, companies that do not take advantage of such worldwide integration will never achieve that unicorn denomination.

One of the main fears for outside investors is that Latin American companies are too niche. Sure, these startups may be able to scale outside of the home country to a few other countries within the region, but the question is, can they scale even further—outside of Latin America?

On the surface, it seems unlikely, especially with these "impact investment" companies and the "niche" industries mentioned earlier in the book. The reality is, however, that 80% of the world's population lives in developing countries. And by 2030, that number is supposed to increase to 85%.[89] Yes, the amount of people living in developing countries is actually increasing! No, that does not mean people are rapidly migrating from developed to developing countries but rather that these developing countries are driving the

---

89 "General Assembly, Special Session." United Nations. Accessed March 22, 2018. http://www.un.org/ga/Istanbul 5/bg10.htm.

ever-increasing global population; the rate of organic population growth in developing countries is growing faster than the rate in developed countries.

I say all of this because chances are many ideas and concepts in one emerging economy can be translated to meet a similar need in another. Now, let's see some real-life examples.

We know FinTech makes up the better portion of venture investment in Latin America, but if we look back at the reasons *why* FinTech thrives and is disrupting the regional market, we could easily just replace the words "Latin America" with "Africa" or "Asia" and the thesis would still hold.

For example, Rafael Hernández at Village Capital recalled his experience working with a company that is in the process of scaling outside its native region. Throughout his time at Village Capital, he continued to notice the ease with which companies that originated in Mexico were achieving scale in places like Chile, as mentioned previously.

When evaluating how to go even bigger, he realized that aside from the cultural similarities, the overall business models were so easily transferable that they really showed no proprietary features that were only applicable to Latin America. In other words, these business models could really benefit anyone. So he began to search and found a company that fits this mold exactly.

Fintual is a robot wealth advisor based in Chile. The company basically utilizes algorithms based on a series of a client's answers to determine the level of financial risk and overall investor profile, which then automatically decide where to invest the money. As Hernández was evaluating the business model, he realized that "the target consumer in this business were the young professionals who prefer to watch Netflix rather than study the market as well as those without access to a traditional wealth advisor."

The FinTech space continues to grow as Latin America develops its financial sector further, so companies like Fintual begin to pop up as a result of these underlying trends. The fact of the matter is that people who prefer to watch Netflix over studying the market do not just exist in Latin America but all around the world, "so the scalability—the problem—is much larger than we think," he claims. In fact, if a startup has the financial resources to expand from Mexico to Chile, then on a purely geographical level, they should be able to do the same in Europe, as the distance is virtually the same.

As Fintual grows, Hernández sees the business soon moving into Asian and African markets. In other words, these impact investments really are applicable outside of Latin America.

With this in mind, think of our previous examples of Tienda Pago and Mexvi; every country has rural areas with corner stores and people in need of homes. It is simply because the need is so prominent in Latin America that these types of companies are popping up there and not in Silicon Valley. Yet, at the same time, the scalability still exists in a similar capacity.

* * *

The scalability of Fintual was based around the overall idea and concept, conceding any cultural issues that may arise when venturing out of Latin America. While I have harped on the idea of the Latin American culture being so distinct and said that due to such peculiarity, venture capitalists are timid to invest or are settling for local alliances, the scalability of a Latin American venture does still exist based off of a cultural play. This might sound completely contradictory to what I have said in previous chapters and even this chapter as well, but a company called Cultura Colectiva, led by Christian Aguirre and his team at Dalus Capital in Mexico City, is affirming such a claim.

Cultura Colectiva is a digital media company centered around providing content to a Latino audience. When

Aguirre and Dalus first invested, Cultura Colectiva only existed in Mexico and a few other Latin American countries. As the company easily diffused its content into the rest of Latin America, "we realized that the large Latino population in the United States would easily empathize with such content," Aguirre says. As a result, Dalus and Cultura Colectiva are beginning to branch out into the United States. In addition, they realized that no other Latin American digital media companies have even dared to venture to the United States, so the company is currently achieving a first-mover advantage in an untapped market.

While there is not a major Latino presence in many places around Asia and Africa, the United States and Spain, have many people who easily identify with the content produced by this company. Similarly, Spain can even serve as a gateway for potential further diffusion into Europe. A lot of impact investments may not have much applicability to the United States or Europe, but at the same time, investments in Latin America are not simply just impact.

Companies like Cultura Colectiva have the advantage of easy scalability due to the nature of their product offering, so venture capitalists are successfully finding areas outside of the region that identify with these types of services.

Following the Cultura Colectiva narrative, Aguirre's firm, Dalus Capital, is part of the Draper Venture Network, created by DFJ co-founder Tim Draper. The Draper Venture Network is an independent web of funds around the world that share best practices, deal flow pipelines, co-investment opportunities, and engage in constructive collaboration to further each other's endeavors.

As Aguirre and his team initially began to do due diligence on Cultura Colectiva prior to investing, they realized they "were not familiar enough with the digital media space to make an informed decision on investing but liked the initial business model. So conveniently, we accessed the network's contact database and simply picked up the phone to speak with a firm in Europe that was more experienced in the digital media industry," he recounts. The European firm actually gave Dalus valuable research and data on the digital media space and allowed Aguirre and his team to learn more about the business model and potential opportunities within Cultura Colectiva that they saw with companies in their European portfolio.

The main point to note about the Draper Venture Network is that Dalus' ability to access the network and receive information on the business model of Cultura Colectiva shows the applicability of a company like this to other parts of the world.

* * *

Of course, scaling outside of Latin America is not that easy—the venture capitalists still do a lot of work.

In the case of Austral Capital, a Chilean-based venture capital firm, managing partner Gonzalo Miranda and his team actively network in the United States for their portfolio companies. When Austral began operations in Chile in 2008, they knew that simply staying in Chile would not bring out the appealing exit options from Silicon Valley and realized that they must branch out to bigger markets.

From the start, they had their eyes on the United States.

Miranda knew these companies could compete abroad; it was just a matter of creating those relationships and getting their name out. After pondering the possibilities for months, they decided to open a small office in California later that year. Over the course of four years, each partner at the firm "spent on average one week per month in California," not just helping initiate operations in the United States but also actively pitching these portfolio companies to other fund managers and learning about best practices for these companies.[90]

---

90   Miranda, Gonzalo. "Venture Capital in Latin America: Connecting Opportunities." Kauffman Fellows. Accessed March

By 2012, many of their portfolio companies like Scanntech, a point-of-sales software for retail stores, had attracted top investors like Sequoia, Motorola Ventures, and Madrona. In fact, Scanntech was Sequoia's first ever investment in a South American company![91]

These particular examples illustrate that these companies can achieve scale outside Latin America, but also reveal to us the biggest obstacle to getting to that unicorn stage for Latin American startups. The difficulty lies not in the business models but in the relationships and in finding a way to get on the global radar.

Dalus Capital and the Draper Venture Network display the early workings of what could be the future of creating a truly global web of venture capital for emerging markets like Latin America.

* * *

Because Latin America has a culture that, for the most part, is so applicable to all of the countries in the region, a startup's

---

22, 2018. https://www.kauffmanfellows.org/journal_posts/venture-capital-in-latin-america-connecting-opportunities.

91 Weyrauch, Sam. "New York Times: Sequoia Capital Turns to South America for Entrepreneurial Investments, including Endeavor Entrepreneur Firm Scanntech." Endeavor. May 25, 2012. Accessed March 22, 2018. https://endeavor.org/in-the-news/nyt-sequoia-capital-scanntech/.

ability to achieve scale and reach a larger target market than its originating country is astronomically higher. This cultural phenomenon is not by any means new; however, as the digital age finally starts to *evolve* the industries mentioned in the first part of the book, this strong connection of cultures is what will allow these technologies to diffuse quickly and within the life of a venture capital fund so that investors have an incentive to actually deploy capital.

I truly believe that the future of connecting emerging markets and allowing the lifestyle of innovation to grow within these countries is through structures like the Draper Venture Network. These types of organizations not only allow investors to make more informed decisions and collaborate on potential investments in certain regions but also allow these startups to expand to other parts of the globe. This is how we can create a truly interconnected, global innovation culture.

CHAPTER 9

GOVERNMENT SUPPORT

———

To make progress on all these goals, it is fundamental we counter the stagnation of recent years, restoring fiscal equilibrium as well as our leadership, dynamism and ability to grow.

— SEBASTIÁN PIÑERA

* * *

2006 marked the emergence of both the startup and "silly name" ecosystem in Mexico.

TechBA, an accelerator and business development program created by the Mexican government and United States-Mexico Foundation for Science (FUMEC), took fifty people on a 2,100-mile journey from Mexico City to Silicon Valley in 2006.[92]

The rationale behind this journey was for these fifty startup founders to experience firsthand the hype and environment of the venture capital headquarters—and to inspire these individuals to unlock the potential of their country.

The outcome of this trip was the Super Happy Dev House series. Despite the strange name, this series of networking events in the Bay Area helped ignite the startup movement in Mexico.

Eventually, a conference called Mexico Web 2.0 in 2008 along with the "Tequila Valley" movement inspired two of the first participants of Super Happy Dev House to create the Mexican.VC accelerator.

In 2012, Mexican.VC was acquired by 500 Startups and still remains a meaningful player in promoting startup development around the country.[93]

---

92 Egusa, Conrad, and Steven Cohen. "Beyond The Maquiladora: A Look At Mexico's Startup Scene." TechCrunch. March 26, 2015. Accessed August 22, 2018. https://techcrunch.com/2015/03/26/beyond-the-maquiladora-a-look-at-mexicos-startup-scene/.

93 Ibid.

The reason the region could create these silly-named movements was because the government started it all in 2006.

Now, the governments across Latin America are beginning to tailor policies and create initiatives that have allowed startups and startup-backing institutions to support founders and technological growth.

* * *

Of course, many emerging markets have their own distinct industries and culture, but what else will allow technology and entrepreneurship to define the future of the region? Why is Latin America, specifically, the emerging market that will experience *supported* startup growth?

* * *

Until recently, one of the main restrictions plaguing the growth of startups in Latin America was access to capital. Many perceive that, historically, venture capitalists did not have confidence in Latin America as a region for entrepreneurial growth and strong exits. Therefore, startups could not develop as a result of this investment deficiency.

But it was not a lack of access to capital for the entrepreneurs—it was the lack of access to the venture capitalists themselves. The local venture capital firms always had faith in the founders, but the limited partners, the ones who ultimately provide the funds, were not as optimistic. As a result, only the wealthy individuals, who could afford to use family money, invested in startups. Even then, due to the protective nature of using family money, investors were not as willing to take risks and generally invested less than sufficient funds or not at all in potentially innovative companies.

As the region develops and successful, scalable companies begin to emerge within the region, fund sizes are starting to grow in a more traditional way like those in Silicon Valley. At the same time, there still lies a slight aura of hesitancy among limited partners, so much of the funding actually hails from government programs seeking to spur innovation and economic growth. Such an injection of fresh institutional capital, however, does not come without extra restrictions and provisions.

* * *

In Chile, a program called CORFO embodies this type of governmental financing. Rodrigo Castro, Managing Partner at Santiago-based Genesis Ventures, has endlessly battled and negotiated with limited partners, but the introduction of this "quasi-capital financing scheme," as he calls it, has allowed him to invest larger tickets in companies like Bolsas Reutilizables.

As for the startup, the founders sought out a mission for a sustainable future, without the need for plastic bags and other products harmful to the environment. The company designs, manufactures, and sells reusable grocery bags to large supermarkets all over Latin America as well as Hong Kong. As Castro analyzed Bolsas Reutilizables, he realized the business proposition was valuable, but they would need a lot of capital to scale and meet demand in manufacturing when partnering with larger clients.

Ultimately, Genesis Ventures decided that the total investment ticket needed was around two million dollars. Unfortunately, using one-twelfth of their twenty-four-million-dollar LP fund in a single Series A round for one company would not have been a good fund fit. Nevertheless, the business was too enticing to pass up.

In came CORFO, an executing agency of government policy for innovation and entrepreneurship. The agency offers lines of credit with a one, two, or three times multiplier based on the amount of LP capital commitment to the company. For every dollar Genesis commits to Bolsas Reutilizables, CORFO will either match, double, or triple the amount, which leads us to the total funding amount needed.

But here is the catch: CORFO is not just free capital. As a line of credit, the commitment essentially works as floating rate debt, usually at LIBOR +1-3%. In essence, CORFO acts similarly to LP commitments in that venture capital firms must pay back the commitment but with interest. While this may seem less desirable than LP funding, venture capitalists only have to return the amount plus interest, which usually comes out to far less than the 80% profit-return requirement to LPs, assuming a typical 20% carry.

Castro could not tell me the exact breakdown, but because of CORFO, "we were able to invest a full two million without upsetting their LP's and leaving significant fund capital for follow-on rounds and other potential portfolio companies," he says.

Initially, Castro and Genesis were only allowed to invest in companies based in Chile, as per the rules of CORFO. Recently, however, the agency has lifted restrictions to allow firms like Genesis to invest in companies based abroad, given that they have a branch in Chile. In addition to spurring entrepreneurial growth in Chile, CORFO has allowed venture capital firms to create a more proven track record with larger investments and show a history of "returning the fund." Through this performance, the institution of CORFO is bringing more LPs to the region, which allows overall fund sizes and investment tickets to grow for venture capital firms like Genesis.

At the same time, Castro asserts, "The introduction of this capital is still not going to create these 15-20x multiples like in the United States, but the frequency of returning the fund and successful exits is much higher."

* * *

While CORFO is specific to Chile, governments around Latin America have instituted similar programs to stimulate national innovation.

In Mexico, Christian Aguirre of Dalus Capital recounted his experience with Structured Equity Securities (CKDs). Instead of direct government capital, the Mexican government loosened past regulation by creating a new vehicle, the CKDs, in which pension funds can invest in certain asset classes. Previously, pension funds could only invest in public companies and federally issued bonds. Structured as a public trust, these CKDs allow pension funds to inject capital into venture capital firms' funds like Dalus Capital Fund II. In fact, the aforementioned fund is entirely a fifty-million-dollar CKD, with a restriction of investing solely in Mexican companies.

With the institution of the CKD and the creation of the new fund, Aguirre and the firm realized that this exponential increase in exposure to capital would allow them to infuse capital into companies that have large scalability potential but also with large asset needs.

Of this fifty-million-dollar fund, Aguirre and Dalus recently invested $6.5 million in Xertica, the largest Google Cloud distribution partner in Latin America, which specializes in consulting for cloud computing services. What they saw in the company, he says, "was the regional play in the advisory services for mid-to-large companies in migrating data from local servers to the Google Cloud, as cloud storage becomes increasingly relied upon for a safer and more reliable data repository." With such a rise in cloud computing, a complementary company like Xertica allows large corporations to shift data with ease.

Nevertheless, as the market grows rapidly so do the needs of the company. Diego Serebrisky, co-founder of Dalus, said, "We are witnessing a rapid transition in all sectors towards cloud services. This transformation is happening globally and at a peculiarly rapid pace in Latin America."[94] By 2020, the global cloud services industry will have a market value

---

94 "Dalus Capital Invests in Xertica – Agencia Orbita." TECH2. February 24, 2018. Accessed March 23, 2018. https://tech2.org/peru/dalus-capital-invests-in-xertica-agencia-orbita/.

of over 203 billion dollars, with Latin America producing an annual growth rate of over 27%.[95] As more and more companies migrate data, Xertica needs a great deal of capital to service these companies simultaneously.

Without the government's new policy on CKDs, Dalus would not have been able to smoothly create this new fund and promptly deploy sufficient resources to Xertica, allowing the company to meet the high demand and scale appropriately. Essentially, the increased availability of capital for the venture capitalists relays downstream to the entrepreneurs and allows these Latin American companies to remain globally competitive.

These government-backed funding policies serve the region in two ways: to create a track record for venture capitalists to demonstrate that they can intelligently handle large amounts of capital and return this investment back to LPs, as well as to foster the swift scalability of companies in the region that require more capital to keep up with global trends.

---

95 França, Vitor. "Why Is Latin America Moving to the Cloud? | LABS." LABS English. June 23, 2017. Accessed March 24, 2018. https://labs.ebanx.com/en/ecommerce/why-is-latin-america-moving-to-the-cloud/.

These funds keep Latin American venture capitalists and entrepreneurs competitive in their own valuable ways and allow the region to constantly continue innovating.

* * *

Accelerators exist all over the world, and in Latin America, they have a profound impact on not only the startups themselves but also the entire economy of a nation or region. Unlike privately funded Silicon Valley accelerators, Latin American governments typically fund these accelerators to spur much-needed growth in the economy.

For the most part, the process of "acceleration" remains the same—startups become part of a cohort, the accelerator potentially puts down a portion of seed equity, offers mentorship and connections, and eventually, these companies graduate with a better business plan and a stronger outlook moving forward. While the mechanism operates in a virtually identical manner, both the need for these programs and the underlying impact have more extensive implications socioeconomically.

* * *

Puerto Rico, recently ravaged by hurricanes, has learned the hard way the necessity of accelerators in terms of developing a global perspective toward business models. As these devastating natural disasters struck the island over the past few years, key flaws have been revealed within the entrepreneurial mindset of the region.

Cyril Meduña serves on the advisory board of Parallel 18, a government-funded accelerator founded in 2016. As businesses began to suffer as a result of the hurricane damages, leaders began to realize this lack of business reach outside of Puerto Rico. Meduña described the entrepreneurs as too insular and said, "People realized, here, that they could not have a business only dependent on Puerto Rico." So he and a team of experienced business leaders started Parallel 18 with the requirement that the companies accepted into each cohort have a global vision.

As the companies in the first couple cohorts began to flourish, in came another problem: United States tax reform. Before President Trump's passing of the new tax bill, the United States actually subsidized industries in Puerto Rico through Section 936 of the Internal Revenue Code, due to their high manufacturing and energy costs, allowing the island to be competitive with countries like China and India. With the new tax bill, the treating of Puerto Rico as a "foreign country" removes the ability for United States companies to keep money in the region without being taxed.

As a result, Meduña and other business leaders have seen multinational corporations that have previously been economically impactful leaving the region. Since the tax reform, Meduña has seen the country's industries taking a look at their businesses and finding a lack of competitive advantage over other nations. "Puerto Rico is losing its ability to compete day by day," he says.

With the retirement of Section 936, the importance of Parallel 18 becomes even more apparent. The impact of Parallel 18 is not to provide capital, but instead the resources to become global. At its inception, the accelerator tapped former Start-Up Chile executive director, Sebastián Vidal, to lead the charge. By having such an experienced leader, the accelerator became an attractive place to grow startups.

As Meduña has witnessed, "companies from all over Latin America come to join the program and when they move to Puerto Rico, these businesses find an abundance of smart and relatively cheap labor in form of programmers and engineers within the island to join and grow these companies." At the same time, they also see Puerto Rico as a stepping-stone to the United States with regard to its roots and cultural affinity with the United States. The influx of these Latin American companies has increased employment within the disaster-stricken country and allowed the economy to obtain much-needed global outreach through the form of these innovative startups, thanks to the presence of Parallel 18.

* * *

Speaking of Start-Up Chile, Andres Araos has seen firsthand through his role as an executive in Start-Up Chile's investors network the importance not only of providing resources to improve business models, but also of the connections that accelerators can bring. As mentioned earlier in our chapter on cultural scalability, one of the biggest issues facing Latin American startups is not necessarily their business models but their lack of network, as well as the challenge of finding a way to create relations with investors and clients outside the region.

In his role at Start-Up Chile, Araos does not necessarily connect the startups to the investors but rather the investors to the startups. I know this sounds like the same thing but rather than publicly marketing startups for anyone to invest in, Araos uses the accelerator's database to send personalized recommendations to each investor based on the startups that best fit the fund. "Essentially, I create individual newsletters for each venture capitalist or potential investor that Start-Up Chile has worked with in the past or has invested in a previous portfolio company. Then, I rank around fifteen startups in the accelerator currently seeking an investment round in each newsletter that best fit the venture capitalist's current fund and industry preferences," he says.

One company that he could not name is currently going through this process and was ranked in a newsletter that went out to a few investors. One potential investor was quite interested in the business but was concerned about the lack of intellectual property over the current product. As a result of this feedback, the startup and the accelerator worked extensively on how to re-mold the product into something more proprietary to secure a patent. The startup eventually obtained the patent and won Start-Up Chile's acceleration program contest for that generation. With the improved business offering, the company is now fielding multiple offers from various investors.

The importance of the accelerator network is that it not only helps connect these startups to investors they previously would not have made relations with, but that it also allows them to obtain this type of feedback to improve their business promptly and go back to work in the accelerator.

The newsletter works both ways in the sense that Araos and Start-Up Chile also become aware of what specific features or aspects of startups that certain investors appreciate. The accelerator can then use this information to improve their mentorship program and help the startups become more attractive to these venture capital firms that want to take these companies global.

*　*　*

The importance of these accelerators is that they understand how to scale these companies globally and know how to formulate them as more attractive to investors. The venture capitalists in Latin America also understand that the accelerators know what they are doing. Subsequently, these investors are more likely to invest in companies that come out of accelerator programs because they have already achieved proven sales and refining of the business. All they need now is the capital.

The accelerators actually make the lives of these venture capitalists much easier in the sense that the investors do not need to get their hands as dirty and worry about the refining of the startup. The investors just need to help scale.

What is most intriguing about institutes like Parallel 18 and Start-Up Chile is that they are government-funded; the policymakers of the countries know that accelerators aids startup growth, which in turn leads to economic growth.

In a sense, venture capitalists can see their investments in these graduated startups as an impact investment because the governments of Puerto Rico and Chile need these accelerator programs to boost the economy. As Parallel 18 seeks to create more global outreach among its cohorts at the same time that the island of Puerto Rico needs more global competitiveness, the accelerator helps alleviate the concerns of both the government as well as a stigma surrounding Latin American startups.

In short, Parallel 18 and Start-Up Chile actually serve these dual goals of improving a nation as well as alleviating major concerns of venture capitalists within the region.

* * *

Michael Arrington, founder of TechCrunch, once said, "I'm a creature of startups. For example, I don't want government interference in the startup ecosystem."[96] In today's startup ecosystem in the United States, Arrington contradicts everything I just said in this chapter because the startup climate is fully cultivated; the venture capitalists, the founders, they have the method figured out. Neither wants the government meddling in their business.

---

96 Arrington, Michael. "If America Was A Startup We'd All Quit." TechCrunch. February 22, 2013. Accessed March 23, 2018. https://techcrunch.com/2013/02/22/america-startup-quit/.

At this point in the lifecycle, government equals regulation. And regulation equals limitation. And limitation equals lowered returns.

In Latin America, this is by no means the case. In a young environment, startups need governments and governments need startups.

The best way for a young ecosystem to mature in the fastest possible way is to have the most powerful institutional body on its side facilitating growth. As Latin American governments continue to sponsor innovation and entrepreneurs in the region, the structural hindrances that could hold back a company or an investor dwindle exponentially.

The best way for a nation to become autonomous and prosperous is through entrepreneurs and the creation of local powerhouse businesses. Every government is looking for that crown jewel company they can call their own. These companies can't just appear—they need to be created. The governments in Latin America are finally beginning to realize that.

CHAPTER 10

INVESTOR SUPPORT

Gato con guantes no caza ratones.
—COMMON SPANISH SAYING, MEANING "A CAT WITH GLOVES DOES NOT HUNT MICE."

* * *

At Axon Partners Group, Luis Castañeda, head of the global firm's Latin American investments, decided to invest in a company called Neumarket once he realized that he could personally aid the company to a feasible exit.

Neumarket is the largest online store for tires across Mexico and Colombia. While the play is very niche, Castañeda saw not the rise of e-commerce as the inherent value but the product itself: the tires. From a rudimentary point of view, the investment seemed like a play on the global growth of e-commerce, but Castañeda felt that channel-based investments are not sustainable.

In his evaluation, at the end of the day, he mentions, "People care about the product they buy and not necessarily where they buy it from." Tires, specifically, have not evolved industrially in recent times around the region so wholesalers continue to purchase tires from companies like Neumarket because of the high and frequent demand. Castañeda says, "People are not aware where to buy a tire until they really need it, and when they do realize the need, they simply just go to the nearest store."

As Castañeda analyzed the company initially, he did not want to invest unless they could create a proprietary brand with a number of partnerships within the next two years. While it might seem difficult to create these kinds of partnerships organically, Castañeda personally has many contacts within the tire wholesaler industry, as he had worked with these companies at Axon and at previous jobs. "I knew that my connections could bring a strong exit opportunity that other venture capital firms could not," he says. As a result of this exclusive value, he and Axon were actually able to receive a discounted valuation on Neumarket because the company knew that their firm was the best strategic partner, no matter how much capital other venture capital firms offered.

Within the Latin American tire industry, there really is no previous signaling or comparable examples to where a company such as Neumarket can end up in five years—IPO, acquisition, or bust. Castañeda and Axon alleviate these concerns through their connections and actually provide a practical solution for exit, ultimately allowing them to invest and attain the extra valuation benefit.

* * *

Around the world, the most important source of value venture capitalists can bring to a portfolio company is not necessarily the capital and the financial resources—it is their understanding of the industry and how they can strategically build the company higher. Anyone could blindly throw millions of dollars at a company and hope the founders know what they are doing with it.

But the idea that capital solves all business problems is mistaken.

A company could pitch to any person with a lot of money, but the reason that they go to venture capitalists is because of the knowledge and added value they, as individuals, can bring to the business. The whole reason venture capital firms can raise such large funds is because these limited partners have the confidence in the individual people at the firm to operate a business appropriately.

Venture capitalists need to bring more to the table than just money.

In Latin America, the individual venture capitalist the startup partners with matters immensely. As startups begin to truly thrive and entrepreneurial opportunities continue to blossom, these flowering companies need a path to exit in an unfamiliar environment. In the United States, it is quite easy to find the most logical path to exit given what preceding companies that have operated in a similar space have done.

In Central and South America, the venture capitalists spend a lot more time prior to investing in understanding a viable exit plan for the startup.

* * *

As mentioned earlier, the individual venture capitalists matter a lot for the entrepreneurs strategically. On the other hand, LPs scrutinize the venture capitalists as well when deciding to invest in a fund, especially in Latin America.

Christine Kenna at IGNIA Partners realized that in order to raise sizable funds, she needed to convince larger, more prominent institutional investors to provide capital. In raising IGNIA's first fund, she and her partners realized they had no previous track record to include in the pitch book, and given general uncertainty and aversion toward the Latin American market, they realized that there needed to be some form of added value that they could bring to not only the startups but also to the LPs providing the fund.

"Some of our potential investors like George Soros, J.P. Morgan, and the IDB Development Corporation hold firms like us to higher standards in transparency when providing capital in the sense that they require more oversight and updates to our operations and portfolio companies," she mentions.

Kenna began to realize that these potential impact companies like Mexvi, for example, might not have the most rigorous and official financial reporting standards and knew that these big-name investors would not tolerate shoddy numbers. In order to mitigate such a conflict, IGNIA actually set up a subsidiary called IGNIA Shared Services, which essentially acts as an outsourced CFO to these portfolio companies so that their books are up to date and standardized, guaranteeing proper accounting standards and best practices.

As a result, the aforementioned institutional investors did, in fact, supply capital to IGNIA's first fund.

Kenna and her team needed to prove why they were the best venture capital firm in Mexico for these LPs to supply capital to; they knew they needed to bring something extra. Should IGNIA not have set up this subsidiary, they might not have been able to raise the fund from these American investors. Not only does the accounting practice help their portfolio companies run smoothly, it also helps the LPs in attaining confidence in IGNIA and ultimately allowing the venture capital firm to raise these larger funds.

* * *

While businesses within Latin America have strong potential for scalability, as discussed earlier, the extent to which the venture capital firm can reach globally plays a strong part as well.

At Genesis Ventures in Chile, Rodrigo Castro elaborated on the how the global expansion of his firm specifically has helped a portfolio company reach new markets by what he calls "smart money." InstaGIS, a San Francisco-based software-as-a-service company that provides predictive mapping for businesses to communicate with communities on a larger scale, is a direct beneficiary of Genesis's expansion.

Although the company is U.S.-based, Genesis was involved from the very beginning, as InstaGIS set a goal to become a global company and tested the waters in Chile initially. Commercial sales performed well, and now, the startup wants to increase its reach. While they partnered with a venture capital firm initially, doing so again in different regional markets would continue to dilute the founders' equity, so they knew from the start that they wanted to join forces with a venture capital firm that had a more international reach by itself.

Castro always knew that, as a fund, he wanted to reach more locations outside of Latin America. Recently, Genesis launched new hubs in Miami and Berlin to take advantage of the startup scene in those areas. At the same time, because of these new locations, the partners situated in these hubs have utilized their connections and allowed InstaGIS to achieve commercial and federal sales in these regions. "As a result of our expansion, the soft landing of these companies has become our responsibility," says Castro.

While Latin America is a reasonable and sizable market for these startups, many entrepreneurs are finding it easier to partner with venture capitalists that have a more global reach so that they can use these connections to scale their businesses further.

* * *

The reason why "getting your hands dirty" with companies is more necessary in Latin America rather than in United States is because, once again, the startup ecosystem is still small.

"If you are founding something in Palo Alto, you just go to University Avenue to any coffee shop, open your laptop, and you turn around and start asking questions about how to do this and how to do that to the guy sitting next to you, and chances are, everybody there is going to be a tech entrepreneur. Here [in Argentina], if you go to a Starbucks, there is basically zero chance that you will find someone that fits your profile," says a famous Buenos-Aires-based entrepreneur turned venture capitalist who requested anonymity. "There simply are not enough places to get advice from third parties."

The operating expertise in Latin America really all lies with those in venture capital.

In Latin America, increasing emphasis on the venture capitalists' getting their hands dirty with their portfolio companies has emerged due to the LPs' higher level of risk aversion and a lack of clear exit paths. Entrepreneurs really want to partner with the firms that have the best connections to exit and scale, as it is much harder for these companies to do so based off the business model alone. Venture capitalists in Latin America must prove to not only the startups but also to the LPs that they can become more entangled in the operations of their portfolio companies to obtain these deals and eventually reach a reasonable exit in this specific market.

*　*　*

While it is important to become more involved with the portfolio company for venture capitalists to demonstrate their experience and build a reputation, startups in emerging markets need all the outside support they can get, whether it be from the government or from their investors.

It is the little things like setting up a more formalized accounting service or helping portfolio companies reach a more global audience. Obviously, investors first and foremost care about returns, but when these investors have the experience and willingness to take the extra step in helping their portfolio companies, that is how the region's companies can achieve greater reach.

The idea of being hands-on with portfolio companies is not unique to Latin America; investors in the developed markets do so too. In fact, this operational involvement is arguably the most important part of venture capital.

The point of this chapter and this factor of the Rishi method is that Latin America checks off this box—not that it is unique to the region.

In evaluating a region to be the place where the next tech boom will occur, it is not always the startups and the industries that require intense scrutiny. Assessing those on the outside is important, and the competency of the surrounding institutions, policies, and venture capitalists plays a significant role in molding the future of the economy.

Latin America has the beginnings of those external factors.

CHAPTER 11

ALTERED STRATEGIES

Many years later, as he faced the firing squad, Colonel Aureliano Buendía was to remember that distant afternoon when his father took him to discover ice.

— GABRIEL GARCÍA MÁRQUEZ,
ONE HUNDRED YEARS OF SOLITUDE

* * *

"75 percent of venture-backed companies never return cash to investors."[97]

---

97 Hoque, Faisal. "Why Most Venture-Backed Companies Fail." Fast Company. January 05, 2014. Accessed March 24, 2018. https://www.fastcompany.com/3003827/why-most-venture-backed-companies-fail.

Such a statistic holds true in the United States, according to an extensive study by Shikhar Ghosh of Harvard Business School after conducting research over a six-year span on over 2,000 companies that raised at least one million dollars in venture capital.

This is the dark side of venture capital we do not hear about. We always hear about the big exits—the Snapchats, the Zyngas, the AppDynamics, etc.—but we do not hear about the multitude of companies that prominent venture capital firms fail to exit and are ultimately forced to liquidate.

* * *

Every budding economy will have hurdles and hoops to jump through; it is never as smooth as it could be. But we all know that.

In my research, not only did I set out to see what was going right in Latin America, I also wanted to see what the limitations were—what were some of the major flaws in the system. But at the same time, I did not want to just witness these foibles as a matter of fact, I needed to see how the players in this game adapted to such shortcomings as well as the ways in which people were really understanding how to participate in this young ecosystem. And if the greatest drawbacks were withstandable and malleable, then I knew that nothing could repress this region in the future.

The question is: are there ways to embrace the fallibilities of such an immature ecosystem? If so, how can we accustom our mindset and invest accordingly in this current state?

* * *

As Esteban Velasco of Velum Ventures says, "The mindset in the United States, especially in the early stage, is more of a 'spray and pray' approach because they know nine out of ten of those companies will fail, but the one that does succeed will have the capacity to return the whole fund and more." Naturally, as the volume of startups remains infinitely higher in the United States, the ecosystem is larger for M&A and IPO activity.

In Latin America, the approach that investors take is a different ballgame. "The approach of a VC in Latin America should be more like one of taking less risks in the technology or product, but, yes, taking risks in terms of the market," claims Velasco.

One example of a company that Velasco currently advises in his portfolio at Velum is Merqueo, an online platform for grocery delivery in Colombia. From Merqueo's perspective, they still see the funding as a traditional, early venture capital stage, as Velasco sits on the board of the company and actively uses his network to advance the business.

From Velasco's perspective, he looks at investments from more of a private equity approach, not in the way he operates the company but rather in his analysis of risk, numbers, and return expectation.

When Velasco first heard the company's pitch at his office, he recalls, "They came to us with an Instacart approach." As Velum began to understand that if the company would make a similar profit to Instacart, he realized that in order to make a decent return as a venture capitalist, Merqueo would need to make millions of transactions per month through using the commission-based revenue model. There was no way they could focus more on the delivery aspect of their business.

After the founder concluded his pitch, he and his team immediately began to run the numbers on potential returns via certain exits to different strategic partners. The only difference from typical venture capital numbers is that when he looked for a satisfying return, he looked for an IRR and cash-on-cash multiple suitable for private equity: 15% – 25% and 3x – 4x, respectively.

Because of the lowered expectations on return, Velasco took less risk. When looking at Merqueo, though they were in their first round of funding, he looked for an already established strong business model—does the service actually work? Do they have credible sales? Etc. So in looking at Merqueo, he looked at the company in terms of a traditional private equity company in the sense that he wanted to make sure the product offering was already well initiated, and that the company just needed to work to enlarge the market to which it sold.

But when analyzing the numbers, he began to foresee Merqueo as a company tailored more toward the online grocery value rather than the delivery. Ultimately, Velum invested in logistics; they invested in inventory. From the use of funding, Merqueo now has the warehouse, Merqueo has the relationships with brands like Nestle and Procter & Gamble, and they do not need to go to Target to buy the groceries—Merqueo is the grocery. There was no need to develop the technology and take that kind of risk; Velasco took more of a risk on developing the market segment in which Merqueo operated. In just the second year of operation, Merqueo boasts a solid revenue of $20 million, according to Velasco.

* * *

With Velum's approach to Merqueo, the risk Velasco took was more of a late-stage venture capital investment to private equity approach, as there was no tweaking of the technology, just more on the operational and efficiency side.

Of course, there are still plenty of venture capitalists willing to gamble on potential boom or bust technologies in the region, but the mentality taken by Velasco is much more prominent for early-stage investors in Latin America.

In Velasco's current fund, which is toward the later stage of its lifecycle, he analyzed over one thousand companies and invested in seven. Four of those seven have already given Velasco successful exits.

So as we can see here, venture capitalists in Latin America, arguably, analyze smarter and not through a "spray and pray" approach. The distinction of the startup scene in this region is that it has more exits with not as spectacular returns, rather than fewer exits with those one or two companies killing it. At Velum and many other firms in Latin America, it is more about getting two-thirds of the portfolio exited with a 3x – 4x return within five years, rather than ten or twenty percent exited with a 10x – 20x return within seven to ten years as in the United States.

Such an example provides us with the methodology for how we can look to invest in Latin America currently.

* * *

Colombia, Brazil, Argentina, Mexico, and Chile are widely understood to be the major players in the Latin American venture capital industry, but there is one forgotten country that has a completely different dynamic: Venezuela.

In the middle of a drastic economic crisis, the country, on the surface, seems like an absolute black hole for investors of all kinds. Venezuela has implemented capital controls to prevent outward capital flight due to the hyperinflation that has plagued the economy in recent years.

As a result of such capital controls, multinational corporations are finding it difficult to repatriate funds from their Venezuelan subsidiaries to their home nation. In addition, the lack of economic growth hinders possibilities of reinvesting this cash flow into plausible, fruitful projects. Essentially, this cash is trapped within the country. Luis Alfonzo, an analyst at Evolvere Capital, learned that the managers of these multinational firms are finding that operating businesses in Venezuela is "too hard, too complex, and too small." It is just not worth the time or the resources.

With these profits virtually useless, multinational corporations are fleeing the country and leaving behind their subsidiaries. These stagnant subsidiaries, with no parent company to guide them and provide financial and strategic resources, have been virtually hung out to dry. These subsidiaries are known as "corporate orphans."

So where does venture capital come in? The aforementioned Evolvere Capital is a venture capital and private equity firm, the first in Venezuela. The state of venture capital in Venezuela is not one of growth, as we know it, but rather one of late-stage investments in these corporate orphans.

For example, take Bridgestone, the tire company based in Tokyo, Japan. In 2015, the company announced the deconsolidation of its Venezuelan operations, Bridgestone Firestone Venezolana C.A. (BFVZ), due to the economic reasons previously mentioned. Luis Alfonzo mentioned this abandoned subsidiary was a company that Evolvere was working with post-deconsolidation. Evolvere injected fresh capital from a fund into BFVZ and essentially restarted the company from the ground up. In other words, BFVZ became a new greenfield investment. As a result of the restored operations, BFVZ was eventually sold to Grupo Corimon, a Venezuelan company focused on the production and commercialization of industrial goods.[98]

---

98 Bridgestone. "Bridgestone Americas Announces Divestiture of its Venezuela Operations to the Corimon Group." News release, May 23, 2016. Accessed March 24, 2018. https://www.bridgestoneamericas.com/en/newsroom/press-releases/2016/bridgestone-americas-announces-divestiture-of-its-venezuela-oper.

When Evolvere restarted BFVZ, they did not help develop any new or emerging technologies or products, like traditional venture capital. What they did was more of a "cleaning up" of the company, such as hiring new managers and efficiently reopening operations at the plants. The value that Evolvere actually brought to BFVZ was more like how a private equity company in the United States would repair a lagging but well-established business.

So how is this not just private equity? While the business itself was turned around like a private equity-owned company, we now delve into the mechanics of what defines venture capital. What defines the differences between angel, venture, and private equity capital is where the funds are coming from, rather than the stage of capital injection.

Even though these forms of financing are typically associated with certain stages of a company, it is how the investor receives the capital to invest that distinguishes angel from venture from private equity. An angel investment is from the investor's personal money, a venture capital investment comes from a fund of limited partners (LPs), and private equity capital, though still from a fund, is raised primarily through taking on substantial debt to buy out a company. In this sense, what Evolvere did for BFVZ was still done through a "venture capital" investment.

These kinds of operations illustrate the state of venture capital in Venezuela—a more backwards approach to growing companies. Rather than growing early-stage tech companies for the first time, investors are *re-growing* mature companies with a path to exit centered around a future acquisition and creating returns for their LPs in that regard.

There is no innovation—no startups. It is just rebuilding.

* * *

Well, there are still startups. Juan Pedro Silva is a Venezuelan entrepreneur and the founder of YEiPii (pronounced "jay-pee"). After graduating from college in the United States, Silva moved back to Venezuela and began working for an insurance company called Seguros Caracas. As a treasurer within the company, he experienced the financial environment of Venezuela firsthand and saw a lot of problems but also a lot of opportunities.

"I always knew that I did not want to be in a corporate job for the rest of my life, and from my work experience, I began to connect the dots and saw the gaps in the market and the opportunity to create something the citizens of the country badly needed," says Silva. After three years at Seguros Caracas, he left his job and launched YEiPii.

Basically, YEiPii is a web application that serves as an intermediary between banks and users. Customers create an account within the application and execute a national wire transfer to the application, which then creates a virtual credit in the account. YEiPii users can then transfer these credits to and from each other via the app. Users can then transfer these credits to their bank accounts. Essentially, "YEiPii serves as a Venmo for Venezuela," Silva says. The difference, however, lies in the fact that a transfer must come from credits within the app rather than an automatic charge to a user's bank account, as with Venmo, due to various limits imposed on Venezuelan banks and the products they can utilize for services.

The application eliminates the need for cash and point-of-sales machines in an environment plagued by hyperinflation. In this cash-strapped country, bank notes essentially become useless day-by-day with inflation.

What is important here is that even the startups are centered around rebuilding the broken economy. As Silva says, "Times of crises are times of opportunities."

While working in the crippled financial sector, Silva saw a huge hole to fill and found the moment to pounce. He knew that if the economic conditions had not persisted and corporations had not seen the mass exodus away from Venezuela, chances are Venmo and PayPal would already exist in the country, leaving him with no possibility of launching YEiPii. While it is not a new, candy technology, it is still something with a sizable, addressable market and is scalable.

As mentioned earlier, there still is no presence of venture capital for these types of ventures in Venezuela. In fact, the people who are starting these companies do not even need the capital. When Silva created YEiPii, capital raising was not a big problem because he and his family had United States dollars saved up, as Venezuelan bolívares are basically useless. In Venezuela, the entrepreneurs that have dollars have no need for outside investments; just having a few dollars can go a long way.

In this aspect, Silva mentions, "Venture capitalists in Venezuela have no need to look at 'startups' because chances are those who can even get off the ground in the first place have ample cash on hand."

He found it much easier to launch an idea in Venezuela because in the United States, chances are there are 500 other people with the same idea all begging angel investors and venture capitalists for capital to outpace each other. When he launched in Venezuela, he had no competition—no need for outside capital.

Venezuela provides an interesting conundrum to the venture capital and startup system we know today; it truly is a complete 180. The startups do not need investment—the corporations do.

* * *

Over the course of around three months, I participated in the undergraduate division of the Global Venture Capital Investment Competition (VCIC). I say global because the more famed and historic MBA competition is actually global with universities from Europe and Asia participating in the event at the University of North Carolina at Chapel Hill. However, the undergraduate division is more "national," as the competition, at that point in time, only consisted of American universities, but the "global" prefix still ended up trickling down to the newly started undergraduate competition.

Representing Georgetown University, the task of our group of five was to act as partners at a made-up venture capital firm and decide on investment in one of three real startups against five other universities. Such a project included receiving pitch decks to research the companies forty-eight hours prior to the competition, and eventually creating a term sheet for investment in one of the companies after due diligence sessions with the entrepreneurs on the day of the event. After winning the Mid-Atlantic Regional Competition in Washington, D.C., our team advanced to the national competition against the other regional winners at the aforementioned UNC-Chapel Hill.

The competition really gave me a better idea of how to really be a venture capitalist and what the nitty-gritty of the job entails. And no—I am not just talking about the fact that we even had to dress like venture capitalists in the tacky blazer-with-jeans dad outfit. I am talking about learning the more technical and negotiation aspects of venture capital aside from simply the qualitative aspects of evaluating and investing in startups.

After our due diligence sessions with each founder, we scurried back to our study rooms to draft a term sheet for the "partner meeting," where we discussed our choice with the judges, who acted as our limited partners and were real-life venture capitalists. To a certain extent, I definitely learned a lot about analyzing companies from a venture capitalist's point of view, but at the same time, being exposed to and actually structuring terms like liquidation preference, pro-rata rights, and valuation cap helped me understand the various technical aspects to these kinds of investments.

I am naturally a "numbers guy." I usually enjoy the quantitative side to things and looking into the financials and valuation, so instinctively, I actually became quite fascinated with crafting the term sheets and learning about how each term affects the deal.

In that regard, I want to discover how these conditions change in a region like Latin America. So let's see how some these term sheet provisions are unique in Latin America.

* * *

Given that the ecosystem in Latin America is so young, it is much harder for both entrepreneurs and investors to accurately value companies because there are so few comparable companies, very few precedent transactions, and generally, no strong history in valuing early-stage companies.

Typically, valuations tend to be lower in Latin America as opposed to in the United States, as investors will justify such a reality due to "risk," which for the most part is true—but another large, underlying reason is that venture capitalists know that they have a monopoly on the "operating experience." In that regard, they can afford to give discounted valuations when negotiating a term sheet because they know that the entrepreneurs need their expertise and capital.

One entrepreneur turned venture capitalist, who asked to maintain anonymity, says, "In Latin America, the term sheets are not as friendly as in the States." At the firm he currently works for, he and his partners maintain a focus on being founder-friendly advisors. However, prior to this company, he used to work for another firm that was not so friendly to the entrepreneurs.

"Over time, we have seen VC's shifting as the environment matures, but at my old firm, some of my partners were pretty ruthless," he recalls. There was one instance where he and his partners were evaluating an upcoming startup that offered language-learning services, and the young entrepreneur was relatively inexperienced in operating a company but nevertheless had a promising idea and strong platform. "I really liked the business, and so did my colleagues, but they took advantage of this young kid when it came time for the term sheet," he mentions.

When he and his partners sat down with the recent college graduate, they began to go over the term sheet line by line, and one thing that really sparked some debate was the liquidation preference.

A liquidation preference, depending on how it is structured, just means what multiple of the original investment the investor will get at exit. Typically, the industry standard is 1x, which seems inefficient, but within a liquidation preference, the standard is "straight preferred," which is the most founder-friendly and means that the investors have the option to receive the multiple of their investment stated or receive the value of the exit amount based on their equity ownership. Investors, for obvious reasons, would hope that the exit is such that they will always just utilize the latter option. There are other ways of structuring a liquidation such as "participating preferred," but "straight preferred" is the simplest and most common.

As I mentioned, when it came time to discuss the liquidation preference, this venture capitalist's partners were lobbying for a 4x multiple! Such a multiple would never be accepted by an entrepreneur in the United States, nor even proposed to begin with, but the Latin American venture capitalists knew they had the upper hand—they knew the kid needed them both financially and strategically to succeed.

"After some arguing, the guy eventually said yes to the 4x, and it was at that moment I realized I was becoming the villain that society sometimes paints us [venture capitalists] to be, and I did not want to be perceived that way. I really love what I do, but I wanted to do so with more of a goal of innovating the region rather than just focusing on the money and our returns."

Eventually, he moved to his current, more amicable firm after this negotiation, but the important takeaway here is that venture capitalists get away with such egregious terms simply because they can.

I am not really sure how you all reading will perceive this—maybe you are in the same boat as our interviewee and realize that hopefully something needs to change, or maybe you are a potential venture capitalist licking your chops and cannot wait to start investing in Latin American startups after hearing about what greedy yet lucrative terms entrepreneurs are willing to accept. Either way, I believe it is important to point out that, at this point in time, this is how it really goes down behind the scenes.

* * *

On the other hand, venture capitalists do not always willingly include such provisions. Rodrigo Castro of Genesis Ventures spoke about his experiences with the shareholder's agreement (another word for term sheet) and how venture capitalists are essentially forced to include specific conditions in the term sheet by their limited partners.

"When we raise a fund, in addition to signing the normal agreements with our limited partners, they place certain conditions on us. They ask for specific liquidity provisions and exit provisions as well as that we have more governance in our companies because they are more risk averse," mentions

Castro. Some of these exit provisions, in his experience, have included restrictions on minimum valuation at sale and even that Genesis must own a certain equity portion at exit. In terms of governance, Castro mentioned that, many times, his LPs have required Genesis to take a majority position on the board of directors of their companies so that they have the decision-making power. "Other than that, 80% of the terms are the general Silicon Valley standard provisions."

If you look at many big venture capital firms around the world, they all have the one person whose position is "General Counsel" i.e. the lawyer or person that drafts all the legal documents. In any deal, legal documents ultimately provide the terms of the agreement and are the "be-all and end-all" of the negotiation. While every venture capital deal has various kinks legally, for the most part, the structure and the process of navigating the deal from a legal standpoint is pretty straightforward. In Latin America, however, it is much more complicated.

"When we first started, we tried to take the legal documents you would see in Silicon Valley or Boston and adapt them to the Chilean standard and realized we ended up having to completely change everything to fit our laws," says Castro.

Christian Aguirre of Dalus Capital also ran into legal complications when the Mexican firm was investing its first fund, especially when trying to figure out the option pool.

In the shareholder's agreement, an option pool is a staple term, which represents the percentage of company stock that is reserved for the employees, excluding management. A standard option pool negotiated during funding rounds in the United States would be around 10%. Negotiating a higher option pool is good for the venture capitalists for two reasons. The first is that it allows the company to be more attractive to talented potential employees. The second and probably most important reason to investors is that a higher option pool shows that the founders are willing to dilute themselves, allowing the venture capitalists to have more influence in decision-making. In other words, should a founder not want to budge on increasing the option pool from, say, 2% to 10%, this reveals that he or she may be hard to work with and less willing to collaborate with the investors, and may be a "control freak" when it comes time to make big decisions.

"In terms of numbers, it's pretty much similar," mentions Aguirre. So while the option pool is still the standard 10% in Latin America, "it's not easy to go to any lawyer in Mexico and say 'I want to do this employee stock option pool' because there are so many different tax implications and legal implications that makes it difficult to solve; not many lawyers really even know how to do it in the right way."

When Aguirre and his team first started at Dalus, they actually outsourced the coordination of the option pool to a third-party legal team that had experience in this area. After a couple of years, they eventually learned how to structure the option pool properly, hired a "general counsel," and now do so in house.

* * *

All of these technical "issues" in negotiations really all relate back to the fact that the ecosystem is still imperfect; the whole startup scheme is a grand work in progress. Legally, investors like Castro and Aguirre first tried to take the legal frameworks from the United States but realized these terms would not work in Latin America. It is important to understand, however, that this trial-and-error phase is coming to an end, and we are finally witnessing all of these kinks being ironed out.

Concurrently, investors are taking it upon themselves to relinquish this previous perception of them being "villains." While certain matters like debates regarding liquidation preference still will occur to a certain extent, the venture capitalists are becoming more founder-friendly out of their own free will.

As the venture capitalists themselves begin to figure out their own baggage, the entrepreneurs, in turn, become more willing and able to innovate, priming a new founder-friendly Latin America for a sustained and substantial startup boom in the years to come.

*　*　*

There are a multitude of disadvantages in investing in Latin American companies as opposed to American companies. Through these stories, however, we can realize that these disadvantages are traversable. There are ways in which founders and investors are taking advantage of the system and embracing the current state.

In many other emerging markets, the structural factors that hinder an economy are far too great to overcome, whether they be political instability, income inequality, or lack of a free market.

Some of these factors, of course, exist in Latin America, but to an ever-diminishing extent. If we can understand how to navigate the path with these conditions still at play, we can understand the potential this region will have when the economy becomes more developed. Because people are willing to put these differences behind them and continue to help advance this market, such a commitment affirms the claims made throughout this book: those that are directly involved, in some form or another, in the region feel the same as I do. Latin America's future will be digital—and global.

Altering our strategies now and promoting investment in the region will allow the ecosystem to grow and develop into what we know in Silicon Valley.

This tech boom that we are going to hear about is not going to happen once the economy becomes developed; it will happen far before that. Understanding how to maneuver through these circumstances will allow not only established investors or potential founders, but also the everyday individual, to successfully and efficiently become a part of this evolution.

CHAPTER 12

RISKS

If you're not a risk taker, you should get the hell out of business.

— RAY KROC

* * *

While understanding how to steer through the limitations is important, equally as crucial is recognizing what may never be overcome and the potentially perpetual perils. If we truly want to know *how* to invest, we also need to know how *not* to invest.

* * *

I have spoken about how venture capitalists continue to find value in startups through niche industries and "clones" from the United States, but there are certain types of businesses and industries that from both a cultural and economic standpoint will neither succeed nor touch the Latin American venture capital space.

The United States "government is terrible at building and buying technology. I know it, you know it, and the government knows it," says Trae Stephens, a partner at Founders Fund in San Francisco.[99]

Stephens specializes in startups within the government space and remains very critical of the shortcomings of national defense and government-based ventures in recent memory. One area of venture capital that the United States has done poorly with and lacks prior advancement is national defense.

The track record of government-related ventures is misleading, however, as two of the five most valuable private venture-backed companies in the world, Palantir and SpaceX, conduct large chunks of their business with the federal government.

---

99 Stephens, Trae. "Innovation Deficit: Why DC Is Losing Silicon Valley." Medium. March 01, 2016. Accessed March 24, 2018. https://medium.com/@traestephens/innovation-deficit-why-dc-is-losing-silicon-valley-bbd0a5744c4f.

After concluding his role at Palantir and moving to Founders Fund in 2014, Stephens and his colleagues at the fund believed that with the huge successes of Palantir and SpaceX, the search was on for government and defense startups and that it was only a matter of time until they found the next unicorn.

"I spent two and half years just looking around and trying to find something, and I came up with nothing," Stephens says of his search. He realized that once you go down the list of the most valuable private venture-backed companies past Palantir and SpaceX, there is "literally nothing" that involves the government or defense. Well, he found some companies—just nothing worth investing in and nothing to sustainably win defense contracts.

After his disappointing search, he went out and co-founded Anduril Industries with Palmer Luckey, co-founder of Oculus VR. Anduril applies virtual reality to help real-time battlefield awareness and other defense-centric industries. The company, in his experience, is really the first startup to gain traction with government partnerships and relationships.

Due to the lack of adequate government innovation, Stephens and Luckey took it upon themselves to improve the defense space because the Pentagon, CIA, and Department of Homeland Security either have not tried or tried and failed. As

Stephens says, "The Department of Defense has even gone out and said to the public that they 'really suck' at innovation." Stephens and the team at Founders Fund are trying to make up for the federal government's mistakes and privately build innovative defense companies.

So how does this have anything to do with Latin America? It is important to understand that when a country like the United States, which spends over three times as much on national defense than the next highest country, fails so heavily in developing such an industry, chances are that such innovation will not reach nor ever become successful in emerging markets like Latin America.

This is different from a "niche industry" like agritech or mining, because defense is a more macro-level and institutionalized industry in every country. The only countries where a sector like this can thrive are the United States, China, Israel, and Russia because their cultures are ingrained with this type of national priority.

The clones in Latin American countries that contain value will certainly not be appearing in the defense sector anytime soon, given these countries' culture and lack of historical need for the area, as well as the grand screw up we have seen in the United States, where such a sector is paramount to our society.

* * *

From the Latin American investors' point of view, homegrown social applications are not going to flourish anytime soon. Both Brian York and Esteban Velasco of Bassin Ventures and Velum Ventures, respectively, know that they would never invest in a Latin American social application. When they say a social application, they mean something like Facebook, Instagram, Twitter, etc. targeted specifically to the Latin American population.

York is an investor in a dating app called Gravity Group, specifically for people living in South and East Asia. He mentions, "While the company itself, is totally out of the scope of my fund, I saw value in the application because the market in South Asia is mature, unlike in Latin America." In his experience with social applications, he found that these ventures need to raise a lot of money— "A LOT." And even after raising this kind of money, they have to go through iteration after iteration to find a sufficient product-market fit.

The ecosystem is the main driver behind social ventures; in such a young environment, it would simply take far too long to develop and scale. Think about in 2004 when Facebook and other social media applications began to thrive in the United States and take over the world…after over three hundred billion dollars of venture funding had been committed in just an eight-year span![100] From 2011 to 2015, just over two billion dollars had been committed in Latin America.[101]

In Velasco's experience, he sees these investments failing in Latin America because they need to be built from the ground up and only after millions and millions of users will they begin to break even. He knows that every time a social media company pitch deck comes across his desk, these companies will drop like flies—and his intuition is confirmed not long after. In Latin America, as York says and has learned from his investments, "startups that survive are the ones solving genuine, industry problems"—not the candy ideas.

It is important to realize that the United States is just beginning to solve problems in these industries and, even so, slowly. These types of ventures may not "never" reach Latin America, as the beginning of this chapter suggests, but it is important to understand that they will not be gaining traction anytime soon, given the reasons that lead to successful ventures in

---

100 "Value of Venture Capital Investment in the U.S. 1995-2017 | Statistic." Statista. Accessed March 25, 2018. https://www.statista.com/statistics/277501/venture-capital-amount-invested-in-the-united-states-since-1995/.

101 *Latin America Venture Capital: Five-Year Trends.* LAVCA | Latin American Private Equity & Venture Capital Association. LAVCA | Latin American Private Equity & Venture Capital Association. 2016. Accessed March 24, 2018. https://gcase.files.wordpress.com/2016/08/lavca-venture-capital-report-2016.pdf.

an emerging market like Latin America discussed in all of the previous chapters.

These emerging markets still need to develop and focus internally on industries that solve palpable issues facing the region. National defense and social media do not fit the bill.

* * *

I wish I could tell you that investing in Latin America is all fine and dandy—that there are no problems. The reality is, however, that the region is still an emerging market, and it still is, for the time being, harder for entrepreneurs and venture capitalists to make returns based on certain economic and political factors we do not see here in the United States.

Corruption and bureaucracy fuel the political adversity facing startups in Latin America today.

Imagine this: it is 2015, and you are the founder of an innovative, FinTech startup in Ecuador. As one of the lesser-developed countries in the region, you know your newly introduced concept of mobile and online payments has promise and is highly needed to advance your home country.

After hours and hours of beta testing, coding, and negotiating with influential people, you finally manage to break into a government-sponsored pitch competition in Quito. Some of the most talented entrepreneurs and ingenious startup ideas are all competing for one grand prize of $50,000 to further their businesses. But you know you have got this.

You walk up onto the hardwood-floored stage, overlooking an auditorium of over 200 people and deliver the most impactful speech and pitch you have ever given. At the end, people applaud furiously, and two older, male government officials sitting next to each other look at one another and nod in convinced agreement.

Three more startup pitches and a twenty-minute waiting period later, you find yourself holding on oversized check for $50,000, excited and optimistic to soon use it to promote the development and scale of your business.

Just one problem: the check is not exactly real, as it usually is not, and you never actually receive any money. Months of arguing and negotiating go by, and nothing happens. You give up. All the hard work and preparation you put into the pitch virtually amounted to the same as not even going. And the icing on the cake is that you eventually find that the government took the money for themselves and the incumbent party.

Such an event happened to an Ecuadorian company that Juliane Butty of Seedstars worked with at the time. While she declined to name the company, this reality faces many Latin American entrepreneurs on a daily basis—the feeling that the whole system is against them. I know I mentioned that countries like Mexico and Chile are beginning to utilize government-sponsored programs for venture capital funding, but it is little things like this type of corruption and elements like extra taxation that plague startups in the region.

As things improve politically, optimism remains, but for now, it is difficult for these entrepreneurs to rely on grants, and they really can only turn to venture capitalists for capital, leaving them no choice but to give up equity in order to raise money.

While these instances of government corruption may contradict the chapter on government support and the Rishi method, these types of injustices are dwindling.

In 2018 alone, former president of Guatemala Otto Pérez Molina and vice president Roxana Baldetti are being tried for corruption cases; former president of El Salvador Elías Antonio Saca is being tried for corruption and money laundering; former president of Brazil Luiz Inácio Lula da Silva went to jail for corruption; former president of Peru Pedro Pablo Kuczynski resigned after corruption allegations; and former Argentinean Minister of Federal Planning, Public Infrastructure, and Services, Julio da Vida is in jail for corruption charges.[102]

Corruption is not extinct in the region, but Latin America is on its way to reforming this oppression.

* * *

It is not always the bureaucracy, though. In Latin America, venture capitalists see trouble with the volume of startups, the volume of potentially feasible investments—and it begins with the entrepreneurs themselves. It may be the system, it may just be general socioeconomic factors, but there is a severe scarcity of young, trend-setting entrepreneurs.

Andres Araos of Start-Up Chile notes that many of the entrepreneurs he works with are much older and only decide to start a company after ten to twenty years working in the corporate world.

---

102 Petersen, German. "Analysis | Latin Americans Are Protesting - and Throwing out - Corrupt Regimes. Why Now?" The Washington Post. June 01, 2018. Accessed September 6, 2018. https://www.washingtonpost.com/news/monkey-cage/wp/2018/06/01/in-a-wave-latin-americans-are-protesting-and-throwing-out-corrupt-regimes-why-now/?noredirect=on&utm_term=.f8d03446659c.

A startup he currently works with in the accelerator is called Neahtid. Founded by a man named Rodrigo Augosto, the company provides wireless charging solutions and products for mobile devices, which actually is an upcoming technology around the world. Augosto worked in the electricity industry for over twenty years before starting Neahtid. After realizing the cumbersome issue of wired power and the potential for energy transfer without the need of wires, he began to work on creating a radical way for charging devices through electromagnetic induction.

While studying at university in Chile, Augosto always knew he wanted to invent and innovate technologically. After hard years of studying and obtaining degrees in computer science and electrical engineering, he knew that he had all the knowledge capacity to create something radical. However, he was enticed into the corporate web with a high-paying salary and began his career as a programmer for a Chilean bank, leaving his entrepreneurial aspirations behind. He moved around and eventually landed a job in the electrical field.

One day, it all clicked. What if there was a way to take advantage of the wireless trend and revolutionize power in Latin America? After noticing the gap in the region and realizing he had the talent to fulfill these needs, he left his job to begin Neahtid.

Currently in Start-Up Chile's portfolio, Neahtid is looking like one of the strongest companies in the whole accelerator and with the interest of potential venture capital suitors, the company has an optimistic outlook for a big exit.

The point here is that many of the entrepreneurs in Latin America only arise after noticing these gaps within a certain industry after working for over ten years. According to Araos, "the majority of startups in the accelerator are created by entrepreneurs in their forties, who have created some sort of venture that is tangentially related to solving a problem in their previous field of work." While this does not apply to all Latin American entrepreneurs, there is still a large stigma around Latin American youth in the sense that they are pressured into having corporate jobs and "earning their stripes" rather than immediately trying to innovate and make an impact.

A similar issue regarding this tendency is that recent university graduates, who, for example, studied engineering or programming do not have the resources to start their own company or continue developing the product they were working on during their master's or doctoral thesis. "It doesn't work like that," asserts Araos.

The problem is that most of these people are in massive amounts of student debt and do not have the ability to work on projects that require them to obtain equity capital or debt funding on top of the debt they already owe. As a result, these previously entrepreneurial youths have to take up corporate jobs to pay off their debts and gain financial stability.

Subsequently, venture capitalists find it difficult to source the same amount of radically innovative ventures as in the United States due to such a lack of young entrepreneurs. The desire to create and not assimilate has yet to be programmed into the Latin American "system."

* * *

Now, let's talk about what the venture capitalists find the most difficult. The end goal, obviously, is to have that famous billion-dollar exit and return the fund and get rich. We've all heard about the unicorns and the big IPO exits. It is always news when a venture-backed company IPOs because you know that puppy is probably valued at well over a billion dollars.

Facebook. Dropbox. Spotify. Twitter.

We have all heard of these four names—some of the biggest success stories in the history of venture capital. The fact of the matter is that the IPO market in the United States is alive and well for venture-backed companies.

I know that in the time I am writing this book that the trend for companies in the United States is to stay private longer due to the increased flexibility given by the JOBS Act of 2012, which is why venture capital funds these days are raising more and more billion-dollar funds. But the idea is that should a venture capital company justify an investment through a feasible path to exit via IPO, they can.

In Latin America, it is a completely different ballgame. The juicy IPO exit is virtually never an option. It is pretty much always a strategic sale.

At Austral Capital, Gonzalo Miranda commented on the current IPO situation in the United States: "Newsworthy as that may be in the United States, this situation is a permanent reality for Latin America where the IPO market is almost non-existent for venture-backed companies."[103] The issue is that Latin American venture capitalists have limited options when it comes to exit paths.

Let's take a look at a couple recent IPOs in the Latin American market.

---

103 Miranda, Gonzalo. "Venture Capital in Latin America: Connecting Opportunities." Kauffman Fellows. Accessed March 24, 2018. https://www.kauffmanfellows.org/journal_posts/venture-capital-in-latin-america-connecting-opportunities.

Netshoes, a Brazilian-based e-commerce platform for sporting goods, IPO'ed in April of 2017 at around $18 a share and popped up over 68% within the first month, which sounds good, but since that pop, the stock is down over 75% to just under $6 one year later. The company went public at around a $558 million valuation and, and as of October 2018, has a market cap of just $72 million.[104]

While venture capitalists are happy in the sense that they got out and did not leave any money on the table, the decision to go public starts with the entrepreneurs and given track records like Netshoes, they are not as enticed to go that route.

Not all Latin American companies perform poorly post-IPO. Despegar.com, an Argentinian travel-booking agency, has remained quite flat in terms of share price; the stock was up about 0.9% six months after going public. The issue with Despegar.com, while still having a pretty large exit of over $1.7 billion, is that the company raised its first round of funding in 2000 and it did not raise again until 2012.[105] And after a whole 18 years since its first capital raise, the company finally made the big exit, which is almost the life span of two funds!

---

104 "Netshoes (Cayman) Limited Common Shares (NETS)." NASDAQ.com. Accessed October 14, 2018. https://www.nasdaq.com/symbol/nets.
105 "Despegar.com: Funding Rounds." Crunchbase. Accessed March 24, 2018. https://www.crunchbase.com/organization/despegar#section-funding-rounds

Especially in the United States, fund managers want an exit within the life of the ten-year fund. In Latin America, such goals are the same, but the problem is that it takes much longer than a ten-year span for certain companies to finally go public. When the time comes to return the fund, telling LPs to wait another eight years will not sit well with them or other potential LPs for future fund raises.

Through these experiences, Miranda affirms, "without a doubt, the lack of exit markets is one of the main challenges for venture capital in Latin America."[106]

* * *

While Latin America seems very promising as noted in previous chapters, there are still always going to be large limitations for venture capitalists in the region. A multitude of factors come into play—some can change and some require deeper, institutional uprooting, especially politically and systemically, but one thing is for sure: Latin America is evolving, and the region still continues to see increased investment year-over-year, despite these limitations. All I know is that

---

106 Miranda, Gonzalo. "Venture Capital in Latin America: Connecting Opportunities." Kauffman Fellows. Accessed March 24, 2018. https://www.kauffmanfellows.org/journal_posts/venture-capital-in-latin-america-connecting-opportunities.

something is working, and the land is poised for big things in years to come.

Latin America, presently, is a risk.

But it's a risk I am more than willing to take.

CONCLUSION

―

Latin America seemed to be a land where there were only dictators, revolutionaries, catastrophes. Now we know that Latin America can produce also artists, musicians, painters, thinkers, and novelists.

— MARIO VARGAS LLOSA

* * *

In the introduction, I mentioned that as a result of my findings and my claims throughout the book, I now want to take action.

I want to be a part of this Latin American digital revolution.

In looking back at my research and understanding how Latin America is poised to experience massive technological growth in the years to come, I figured out the reasons *why* such growth can be sustainable and scalable.

The four parts of this book encompass how Latin America's future will back up my aforementioned claim, but simultaneously, these four elements comprise a way to determine if any emerging market is primed for vast digital innovation in the future.

And so, I have presented the Rishi method for analyzing the startup ecosystem of emerging markets.

In a sense, these four components are in chronological order of what to look for first. If you can cross the first one off as matching the criteria, then you can move on to the next and so on.

This method can be used for an even more specific scope than one as broad as Latin America. If a certain group of nations, a country, or even a city exhibits these four factors, such an approach will still apply. As long as some geographical sphere contains evolving industries driven by a deep-rooted societal need; cultural friction and emphasis; institutional support; and a demonstrated path to navigating the market's specific, structural limitations, then you can be sure the area will experience some sort of dynamic yet defensible startup boom in the future.

Now, here is where I come in.

My enjoyment with learning about foreign cultures combined with my knowledge of the Latin American ecosystem has led me to desire to make an impact.

With a potential healthy sum of capital, I plan on creating an AngelList syndicate for investing not only in some of the companies mentioned in the book but also for potential investments in other companies that seem promising and fit these criteria.

Yes, the Rishi method can even be used to evaluate a specific company in an emerging market.
- Does the company reside in an industry and operate in a way that serves a genuine need?
- Does the company have local friction points to keep away outside companies?
- Does the company have institutional support from the government, whether directly or through an industry-wide policy? Have investors or other institutions shown a willingness to aid the company?

- Does the company have structural flaws that are mainly a result of its ecosystem rather than its concept? Can I understand how not to operate this company?

In answering yes to all four of these questions, a prospective startup has just satisfied the Rishi method's test for potential investment. Of course, we need to delve deeper into the specifics of the company, its financials, the founders, etc., but these questions serve as an initial analysis of whether or not the startup can remain sustainable not only within its own emerging market but also globally.

Let's pose these questions together—not just in Latin America but also around the world.

I have taken it upon myself to commit to improving the conditions of founders in overlooked countries. Silicon Valley's reign as king of venture capital probably will not end anytime soon, but it is finally time to find the underserved areas that society does not think of—the areas that could catch up to Silicon Valley in the future.

Nobel Peace Prize winner Muhammad Yunus famously said, "All human beings are entrepreneurs."

Everywhere, people have the entrepreneurial spirit, not just in Silicon Valley.

I love learning about the differences between foreign cultures and my own, but one thing is the same across cultures: the entrepreneurial spirit. It may not be as refined as in Northern California, but it is out there.

I have made it my mission to go out and find the regions that are exhibiting the signs of this digital uprising, starting with Latin America. My better understanding of the business world will allow me to intelligently source and invest in these regions of the future.

First and foremost, it will be Latin America, the area and culture I have become so fond of and captivated by since I was young. But afterwards, it could be any developing market around the globe.

Don't just invest in me. Invest in the world.

APPENDIX

Introduction

Chen, Lulu Yilun. "Chinese Investors Bet on Latin America for Next Tech Gold Rush." Bloomberg.com. March 4, 2018. Accessed September 5, 2018. https://www.bloomberg.com/news/articles/2018-03-04/chinese-startups-export-playbook-to-latin-america-for-new-riches.

Gordon, Kyle. "Topic: Internet Usage in Latin America." Www.statista.com. 2017. Accessed September 5, 2018. https://www.statista.com/topics/2432/internet-usage-in-latin-america/.

Mitchell, Caitlin. "Tech Companies Back New Coalition Created by LAVCA to Support Latin America's Record Breaking Startup Growth." LAVCA | Latin American Private Equity & Venture

Capital Association. April 4, 2018. Accessed September 5, 2018. https://lavca.org/press-release/tech-companies-back-new-coalition-created-lavca-support-latin-americas-record-breaking-startup-growth/.

Truong, Alice. "Groupon Is Still the Fastest Company to Reach a Billion-dollar Valuation." Quartz. May 22, 2015. Accessed September 4, 2018. https://qz.com/398090/groupon-still-the-fastest-company-to-reach-a-unicorn-billion-dollar-valuation/.

Yang, Yingzhi. "China's Start-ups Attract Almost Half of World's Venture Capital Investments." South China Morning Post. July 05, 2018. Accessed September 4, 2018. https://www.scmp.com/tech/article/2153798/china-surpasses-north-america-attracting-venture-capital-funding-first-time.

Chapter 1

Pearce, Bryan. *Back to Reality: EY Global Venture Capital Trends 2015*. Ernst & Young. Www.ey.com. 2016. Accessed Summer, 2018. https://www.ey.com/publication/vwluassets/ey-global-venture-capital-trends-2015/$file/ey-global-venture-capital-trends-2015.pdf.

Chapter 2

Bathke, Benjamin. "Insights into Germany's Startup Scene | DW | 18.10.2017." DW.COM. October 18, 2017. Accessed October 13, 2018. https://www.dw.com/en/insights-into-germanys-startup-scene-entrepreneurship-funding-venture-capital-investing-expansion/a-40993536.

Butcher, Mike. "London's Tech Boom Is More Than Just Hype, The Hard Numbers Say So." TechCrunch. September 20, 2014. Accessed September 5, 2018. https://techcrunch.com/2014/09/20/londons-tech-boom-is-more-than-just-hype-the-hard-numbers-say-so/.

Featherstone, Emma. "WorldRemit Founder: 'I Lost My Job to Uncover UN Fraud'." The Guardian. January 20, 2017. Accessed September 5, 2018. https://www.theguardian.com/small-business-network/2017/jan/20/worldremit-founder-lost-job-fraud-money-transfers.

"France Population 2018." France Population 2018 (Demographics, Maps, Graphs). Accessed October 13, 2018. http://worldpopulationreview.com/countries/france-population/.

Hodgson, Leah. "European VC Trends in 8 Charts." PitchBook. July 23, 2018. Accessed September 5, 2018. https://pitchbook.com/news/articles/european-vc-trends-in-8-charts.

Kharpal, Arjun. "Op-Ed: China's Copycat Tech Image Is Fading and That Should Worry US Tech Giants." CNBC. June 13, 2017. Accessed September 5, 2018. https://www.cnbc.com/2017/06/13/china-copycat-tech-image-is-fading-and-that-should-worry-us-giants.html.

Li, Jane. "How China's Consumer Patriotism Is Hitting US and International Brands." South China Morning Post. March 22, 2018. Accessed September 5, 2018. https://www.scmp.com/business/china-business/article/2138267/chinas-young-consumers-are-snubbing-foreign-brands-amid.

Lu, Ariel, Frank Fu, and Jessie Chen. *China's Venture Capital (VC): Bigger than Silicon Valley's?* INSEAD. Www.insead.edu. April 20, 2018. Accessed September 5, 2018. https://www.insead.edu/sites/default/files/assets/dept/centres/gpei/docs/insead-student-china-venture-capital-apr-2018.pdf.

Nair, Praseeda. "Are European Tech Start-ups Being Held Back by Lower 'reward for Risk'?" Growth Business. November 30, 2017. Accessed September 5, 2018. https://www.growthbusiness.co.uk/european-tech-start-ups-lower-reward-for-risk-2553041/.

Nheu, Christopher. "The Secret Behind How Chinese Startups Are Winning – Startup Grind – Medium." Medium. May 01, 2018. Accessed September 5, 2018. https://medium.com/

startup-grind/the-secret-behind-how-chinese-startups-are-winning-44876b196626.

Ranger, Steve. "Startup Republic: How France Reinvented Itself for the 21st Century by Wooing Entrepreneurs to Paris." TechRepublic. Accessed September 5, 2018. https://www.techrepublic.com/article/startup-republic-how-france-reinvented-itself-for-the-21st-century-by-wooing-entrepreneurs-to-paris/.

Roebroek, Sebastiaan. "Growth Story: How German Startup Uberall Became the Go-to Solution for Location Listings." The Next Web. July 05, 2017. Accessed September 5, 2018. https://thenextweb.com/insider/2017/07/05/uberall-growth/.

Russell, Jon. "Alibaba's Lazada Confirms Acquisition of Singapore Web Grocery Startup RedMart." TechCrunch. November 01, 2016. Accessed September 5, 2018. https://techcrunch.com/2016/11/01/alibaba-lazada-redmart-confirmed/.

Schuman, Michael. "Venture Communism: How China Is Building a Start-Up Boom." The New York Times. September 03, 2016. Accessed September 5, 2018. https://www.nytimes.com/2016/09/04/business/international/venture-communism-how-china-is-building-a-start-up-boom.html.

Sharma, Rahul. *London as a FinTech Hub: What Does the Future Hold?* Deloitte. October 25, 2017. Accessed September 5, 2018.

https://events.economia.cz/media/event/17415/files/rahul-sharma_5622d7a.pdf.

Stone, Brad, and Lulu Yilun Chen. "Uber Slayer: How China's Didi Beat the Ride-Hailing Superpower." Bloomberg.com. October 6, 2016. Accessed September 5, 2018. https://www.bloomberg.com/features/2016-didi-cheng-wei/.

"U.S. Population (LIVE)." U.S. Population (2018) - Worldometers. Accessed October 13, 2018. http://www.worldometers.info/world-population/us-population/.

Williams-Grut, Oscar. "Here's Why WorldRemit Is worth £320 Million - It's Building the WhatsApp of Money." Business Insider. June 15, 2015. Accessed September 5, 2018. https://www.businessinsider.com/worldremit-founder-ismail-ahmed-mobile-wallets-moneyconf-500-million-valuation-2015-6.

Wong, Billy. "China's Middle-Class Consumers: Preferences and Spending Trends." China's Middle-Class Consumers: Preferences and Spending Trends | HKTDC. July 18, 2017. Accessed September 5, 2018. http://economists-pick-research.hktdc.com/business-news/article/Research-Articles/China-s-Middle-Class-Consumers-Preferences-and-Spending-Trends/rp/en/1/1X000000/1X0AAQP5.htm.

"WorldRemit: Funding Rounds." Crunchbase. Accessed September 5, 2018. https://www.crunchbase.com/organization/worldremit#section-funding-rounds.

Chapter 3

Balea, Judith. "Southeast Asia Sees Record Startup Funding in 2017." Tech in Asia - Connecting Asia's Startup Ecosystem. January 25, 2018. Accessed September 7, 2018. https://www.techinasia.com/southeast-asia-sees-record-startup-funding-2017.

Bowman, Matt. "Sequoia Raising $1 Billion Umbrella Fund." VatorNews. December 22, 2009. Accessed October 13, 2018. http://vator.tv/news/2009-12-22-sequoia-raising-1-billion-umbrella-fund.

Debusmann, Bernd, Jr. "Middle East Venture Partners: Investing in the Future of Tech." ArabianBusiness.com. January 16, 2018. Accessed September 7, 2018. https://www.arabianbusiness.com/startup/387400-middle-east-venture-partners-investing-in-the-future-of-tech.

Khoury, Souhail. "VC Capital in MENA and Lebanon : Learnings from the Middle East Investment Summit." Medium. May 17, 2018. Accessed September 7, 2018. https://medium.com/@souhailk/vc-capital-in-mena-and-lebanon-learnings-from-the-middle-east-investment-summit-55221c216e31.

Knowles, Daniel. *The 1.2 Billion Opportunity*. The Economist. The Economist. April 16, 2016. Accessed September 6, 2018. http://www.economist.com/sites/default/files/20160416_africa.pdf.

McKemey, Kevin, Nigel Scott, David Souter, Thomas Afullo, Richard Kibombo, and O. Sakyi-Dawson. *Innovative Demand Models for Telecommunications Services*. Department for International Development. September 2003. Accessed September 6, 2018. https://assets.publishing.service.gov.uk/media/57a08d10e5274a27b20015e3/2936_R8069_FinalReport.pdf.

Monks, Kieron. "M-Pesa: Kenya's Mobile Success Story Turns 10." CNN. February 24, 2017. Accessed September 6, 2018. https://www.cnn.com/2017/02/21/africa/mpesa-10th-anniversary/index.html.

Russell, Jon. "Amazon Completes Its Acquisition of Middle Eastern E-commerce Firm Souq." TechCrunch. July 03, 2017. Accessed October 13, 2018. https://techcrunch.com/2017/07/03/amazon-souq-com-completed/.

"South-Eastern Asia Population (LIVE)." Population of South-Eastern Asia (2018) - Worldometers. October 14, 2018. Accessed October 14, 2018. http://www.worldometers.info/world-population/south-eastern-asia-population/.

Zhu, Juliet. "How to Hunt Unicorns in Southeast Asia: Explains a Venture Capitalist – KrASIA." Kr-Asia. June 20, 2018. Accessed September 8, 2018. https://kr-asia.com/how-to-hunt-unicorns-in-southeast-asia-explains-a-venture-capitalist/.

Chapter 5

Hodgson, Camilla. "The World's 2 Billion Unbanked, in 6 Charts." Business Insider. August 30, 2017. Accessed March 20, 2018. https://www.businessinsider.com/the-worlds-unbanked-population-in-6-charts-2017-8.

Kokalitcheva, Kia. "Colombian Startup Rappi Wants to Deliver 'Everything'." Fortune. November 8, 2016. Accessed March 20, 2018. http://fortune.com/2016/11/08/rappi-delivery-latin-american/.

Lunden, Ingrid. "Finance Startup Nubank Nabs $14.3M In Sequoia's First Brazil Investment." TechCrunch. September 25, 2014. Accessed March 20, 2018. https://techcrunch.com/2014/09/25/finance-startup-nubank-nabs-14-3m-in-sequoias-first-brazil-investment/.

"Motor Vehicles (per 1,000 People)." Motor Vehicles (per 1,000 People) | Data | Table. 2018. Accessed March 20, 2018. https://web.archive.org/web/20140209114811/http://data.worldbank.org/indicator/IS.VEH.NVEH.P3.

Penn, David. "Nubank Challenges Brazil's Big Banks in Wake of $150 Million Funding Round." Finovate. March 30, 2018. Accessed August 20, 2018. https://finovate.com/nubank-challenges-brazils-big-banks-in-wake-of-150-million-in-funding-round/.

Price, Dennis. "In Latin America, What's an Impact Investment?" ImpactAlpha. February 10, 2018. Accessed March 20, 2018. https://impactalpha.com/in-latin-america-whats-an-impact-investment-9097cd4aec4d/.

Shieber, Jonathan. "Nubank Is Now worth $4 Billion after Tencent's $180 Million Investment." TechCrunch. October 08, 2018. Accessed October 14, 2018. https://techcrunch.com/2018/10/08/tencent-cash-values-nubank-at-4-billion/.

The Mobile Economy: Latin America and the Caribbean 2017. GSMA Intelligence. GSMA Intelligence. 2017. Accessed March 20, 2018. https://www.gsmaintelligence.com/research/?file=e14f-f2512ee244415366a89471bcd3e1&download.

Chapter 6

BovControl: Funding Rounds." Crunchbase. Accessed October 14, 2018. https://www.crunchbase.com/organization/bovcontrol#-section-funding-rounds

Burwood-Taylor, Louisa. "NXTP Labs Launches First Latin American Agtech Accelerator." AgFunderNews. July 17, 2016. Accessed March 21, 2018. https://agfundernews.com/nxtp-labs-launches-first-ever-agtech-accelerator-latin-america.html/.

Herrera, Clarisa. "Nicolás Szekasy of Kaszek Ventures on Why Local Know-How Is Key." PulsoSocial. December 20, 2013. Accessed March 21, 2018. https://pulsosocial.com/en/2013/12/20/nicolas-szekasy-of-kaszek-ventures-on-why-local-know-how-is-key/.

Homejoy: Funding Rounds." Crunchbase. Accessed October 14, 2018. https://www.crunchbase.com/organization/homejoy#section-funding-rounds

Kendall, Matt. "Argentina Startups Aim at the Agritech Boom ." Nearshore Americas. April 19, 2017. Accessed March 21, 2018. https://www.nearshoreamericas.com/argentina-startups-aim-at-the-agritech-boom/.

"Kilimo - More Yields with Less Water." Kilimo - More Yields with Less Water. Accessed March 20, 2018. http://www.kilimo.com.ar/.

Madden, Sam. "Why Homejoy Failed ... And The Future Of The On-Demand Economy." TechCrunch. July 31, 2015. Accessed

March 21, 2018. https://techcrunch.com/2015/07/31/why-home-joy-failed-and-the-future-of-the-on-demand-economy/.

Schwartz, Ariel. "The 'Internet of Cows' Is Taking over Farms across the World." Business Insider. January 24, 2017. Accessed March 21, 2018. https://www.businessinsider.com/bovcontrol-internet-of-cows-2017-1.

Shaw-Smith, Peter. "Chile Continues Dry Bulk Dominance." Chile Continues Dry Bulk Dominance | IHS Fairplay. April 12, 2018. Accessed April 25, 2018. https://fairplay.ihs.com/bulk/article/4299736/chile-continues-dry-bulk-dominance.

Chapter 7

Dollarama. "Dollarama Enters into an Agreement to Provide Business Expertise and Sourcing Services to Central American Dollar Store Chain Dollar City." News release, February 5, 2013. Dollarama. Accessed August 20, 2018. http://www.dollarama.com/wp-content/uploads/2013/02/Barcelona-release_Feb-5-v014-SEDAR.pdf.

Chapter 8

"Countries in Latin America and the Caribbean by Population (2018)." Countries in Latin America and the Caribbean by Population (2018) - Worldometers. 2018. Accessed October

14, 2018. http://www.worldometers.info/population/countries-in-latin-america-and-the-caribbean-by-population/.

"General Assembly, Special Session." United Nations. Accessed March 22, 2018. http://www.un.org/ga/Istanbul 5/bg10.htm.

"Mercado Libre, NXTP Labs & Alaya Capital Invest in 123Seguro." LAVCA | Latin American Private Equity & Venture Capital Association. December 20, 2017. Accessed March 22, 2018. https://lavca.org/2017/12/20/mercado-libre-nxtp-labs-alaya-123seguro/.

Miranda, Gonzalo. "Venture Capital in Latin America: Connecting Opportunities." Kauffman Fellows. Accessed March 22, 2018. https://www.kauffmanfellows.org/journal_posts/venture-capital-in-latin-america-connecting-opportunities.

"The Lewis Model – Dimensions of Behaviour." Cross Culture. June 22, 2015. Accessed March 22, 2018. https://www.crossculture.com/the-lewis-model-dimensions-of-behaviour/.

Weyrauch, Sam. "New York Times: Sequoia Capital Turns to South America for Entrepreneurial Investments, including Endeavor Entrepreneur Firm Scanntech." Endeavor. May 25, 2012. Accessed March 22, 2018. https://endeavor.org/in-the-news/nyt-sequoia-capital-scanntech/.

Chapter 9

Arrington, Michael. "If America Was A Startup We'd All Quit." TechCrunch. February 22, 2013. Accessed March 23, 2018. https://techcrunch.com/2013/02/22/america-startup-quit/.

"Dalus Capital Invests in Xertica – Agencia Orbita." TECH2. February 24, 2018. Accessed March 23, 2018. https://tech2.org/peru/dalus-capital-invests-in-xertica-agencia-orbita/.

Egusa, Conrad, and Steven Cohen. "Beyond The Maquiladora: A Look At Mexico's Startup Scene." TechCrunch. March 26, 2015. Accessed August 22, 2018. https://techcrunch.com/2015/03/26/beyond-the-maquiladora-a-look-at-mexicos-startup-scene/.

França, Vitor. "Why Is Latin America Moving to the Cloud? | LABS." LABS English. June 23, 2017. Accessed March 24, 2018. https://labs.ebanx.com/en/ecommerce/why-is-latin-america-moving-to-the-cloud/.

Chapter 11

Bridgestone. " Bridgestone Americas Announces Divestiture of its Venezuela Operations to the Corimon Group." News release, May 23, 2016. Accessed March 24, 2018. https://www.bridgestoneamericas.com/en/newsroom/press-releases/2016/bridgestone-americas-announces-divestiture-of-its-venezuela-oper.

Hoque, Faisal. "Why Most Venture-Backed Companies Fail." Fast Company. January 05, 2014. Accessed March 24, 2018. https://www.fastcompany.com/3003827/why-most-venture-backed-companies-fail.

Chapter 12

"Despegar.com: Funding Rounds." Crunchbase. Accessed March 24, 2018. https://www.crunchbase.com/organization/despegar#-section-funding-rounds

Latin America Venture Capital: Five-Year Trends. LAVCA | Latin American Private Equity & Venture Capital Association. LAVCA | Latin American Private Equity & Venture Capital Association. 2016. Accessed March 24, 2018. https://gcase.files.wordpress.com/2016/08/lavca-venture-capital-report-2016.pdf.

Miranda, Gonzalo. "Venture Capital in Latin America: Connecting Opportunities." Kauffman Fellows. Accessed March 24, 2018. https://www.kauffmanfellows.org/journal_posts/venture-capital-in-latin-america-connecting-opportunities.

"Netshoes (Cayman) Limited Common Shares (NETS)." NASDAQ.com. Accessed October 14, 2018. https://www.nasdaq.com/symbol/nets.

Petersen, German. "Analysis | Latin Americans Are Protesting - and Throwing out - Corrupt Regimes. Why Now?" The Washington Post. June 01, 2018. Accessed September 6, 2018. https://www.washingtonpost.com/news/monkey-cage/wp/2018/06/01/in-a-wave-latin-americans-are-protesting-and-throwing-out-corrupt-regimes-why-now/?noredirect=on&utm_term=.f8d03446659c.

Stephens, Trae. "Innovation Deficit: Why DC Is Losing Silicon Valley." Medium. March 01, 2016. Accessed March 24, 2018. https://medium.com/@traestephens/innovation-deficit-why-dc-is-losing-silicon-valley-bbd0a5744c4f.

"Value of Venture Capital Investment in the U.S. 1995-2017 | Statistic." Statista. Accessed March 25, 2018. https://www.statista.com/statistics/277501/venture-capital-amount-invested-in-the-united-states-since-1995/.

Made in the USA
Coppell, TX
24 October 2024